D0875432

THE WIND BLOWS FREE

Books By Frederick Manfred

THE GOLDEN BOWL	1944
BOY ALMIGHTY	1945
THIS IS THE YEAR	1947
THE CHOKECHERRY TREE	1948
THE PRIMITIVE	1949
THE BROTHER	1950
THE GIANT[1]	1951
LORD GRIZZLY	1954
MORNING RED	1956
RIDERS OF JUDGMENT	1957
CONQUERING HORSE	1959
ARROW OF LOVE (stories)	1961
WANDERLUST (triology)[2]	1962
SCARLET PLUME	1964
THE SECRET PLACE[3]	1965
WINTER COUNT (poems)	1966
KING OF SPADES	1966
APPLES OF PARADISE (stories)	1968
EDEN PRAIRIE	1968
CONVERSATIONS[4]	1974
MILK OF WOLVES	1976
THE MANLY-HEARTED WOMAN	1976
GREEN EARTH	1977
THE WIND BLOWS FREE	1979

[1]Mr. Manfred wrote under the name of Feike Feikema from 1944 through 1951.
[2]A new revised version of the three novels, *The Primitive, The Brother,* and *The Giant,* and published in one volume.
[3]Originally published in hardback as *The Man Who Looked Like The Prince of Wales;* reprinted in paperback as *The Secret Place.*
[4]Moderated by John R. Milton.

A REMINISCENCE BY FREDERICK MANFRED C. 2

The Wind Blows Free

THE CENTER FOR WESTERN STUDIES
Augustana College
Sioux Falls, South Dakota
1979

Published by
THE CENTER FOR WESTERN STUDIES
an
HISTORICAL RESEARCH AND ARCHIVAL
Agency of
Augustana College
Sioux Falls,
South Dakota

Illustrations by Elsie Thorson

ISBN: Number 0-931170-09-5
Library of Congress Catalog Number 79-53217
ALL RIGHTS RESERVED
©1979 by Frederick Feikema Manfred
©1979 Illustrations by The Center for Western Studies
First Edition
Printed by Sioux Printing, Inc., Sioux Falls, South Dakota
Manufactured in the United States of America

For my sweet children
FREYA, MARYA, AND FREDERICK

Acknowledgment
To DWAYNE O. ANDREAS
who helped out when I was in need.

Also
In memory of ROBERT SMITH SURTEES.

Frederick Manfred standing beside his old flatbed Ford on the farm just east of Doon, Iowa, August, 1930, at the age of 18.

Frederick Manfred about to graduate from Calvin College,
Grand Rapids, Michigan, spring, 1934.

Frederick Manfred sitting in his cabin study near Luverne, Minnesota, March, 1978. Photo by James Studio.

SPECIAL FACE

I ask for no alms from your pitying hand,
Nor favors from your wind-red lips and your eyes.
The balm that your pitying tears should not lend
Will embitter my rare-made cup of sighs.
And, though I should permit into my warm
Unguarded heart the realism of the soiled
And smoke-greyed homes that love can not reform,
I shall long for your love in my dream world.

I'll ask for no miracles while alive
In my bubble-strong, make-believe trance.
Though my friends should unwittingly contrive
To belittle in my mind your fragance
And defying eyes, my dreams of you, I know,
Will soar over brooks and waste and the snow.

Frederick Feikema
Spring, 1934
Calvin College Dormitory
Grand Rapids, Michigan

FOREWORD

I've often been asked how I got started as a writer.

In my boyhood I didn't have a single friend interested in writing. I didn't study creative writing in college. And I didn't meet a well-known author until sometime after I was published.

At the age of five, though, even before I started the primary grade in a country school in northwest Iowa, I already had the dream of becoming a writer. I had seen in our farm home a slim green volume of privately printed verse written by my father's sister, Kathryn Feikema. Aunt Kathryn lived with us and was one of my very first teachers. She loved me and taught me to read before I started school. She and my mother used to play rhyming games with me while my mother made supper. And once I began school I soon developed into a good reader. My father and my mother used to say of me that they could always find me in one of two places: either exploring the hummocks along the creek in the pasture or sitting on the screen porch with my head in a book.

What really put the heat into my private burning bush was a hitchhiking trip I took in August of 1934, a few months after graduating from Calvin College in Grand Rapids, Michigan. I went to see the Shining Mountains of the Far West. That trip released my soul.

Three years after that trip, on a Saturday, I was invited out to a party at my friend Jim's house. I had by that time, after much wandering, found a job with the Minneapolis *Journal*. Saturday was always a tough day at the plant, from eight in the morning until almost midnight when the final edition of the Sunday paper was put to bed.

I

As I stepped across the street in the dark to get my car out of the *Journal* parking lot, I wasn't too sure I cared to go to the party any more that night. I was pooped.

But my old Dodge fired on the first revolution and soon I was driving across the Washington Avenue bridge over the twinkling Mississippi River. I took a right and followed the East River Road around to Franklin Avenue. The streetlights burned a bright citrine under the black green oaks.

The deep gorge of the Mississippi and all the wonderful trees and the lovely greens along the boulevard made me wish I had a date for Jim's party. It was time I fell in love again. I'd pretty well gotten over a college love and was ripe for a new romance. I wondered if maybe there might not be a new shining girl at Jim's house.

It was quarter past twelve when I eased the Dodge up Prospect Hill. When I got near the top I saw that the lights were still on in Jim's house. Good. The party was still going. I parked my car on a side street and walked around the side of the house and entered by the back door into the kitchen. Two strangers, a man and a woman, were talking politics by the sink. They'd each just opened a fresh bottle of beer. I pushed through the swinging doors into the living room. It was full, some twenty people, all talking at once about the President. I knew only five people there, Jim and his wife, Laura, a widow social worker, Mac, a man from the Department of Education, and Starke, a psychologist from the University of Minnesota. I settled on the floor near Jim.

The argument about the President was pretty well divided. Some thought the President's liberal program was going to win out and lick the Depression; some thought he was going too slow and should be more radical. Looking around I noted no one was drinking hard liquor. Just beers or cokes. There never were orgies at

II

Jim's house; just wonderful good talks by people dedicated to do some kind of social good. High class people. All college graduates at least. I liked them. And I always learned something just sitting around listening to them.

Pretty soon Jim noticed me. "Where's your beer?"

I lifted a shoulder. "There an extra bottle for me?"

"Of course. In the icebox. Help yourself."

I gathered myself up on my legs and wandered out into the kitchen. The couple there had quit talking about politics and were busy smooching by the door. They broke apart and smiled sheepishly. I wondered a little about them. They were probably only sneaking a kiss in the kitchen while their spouses were arguing politics in the living room. I helped myself to a Jordan beer and returned to the living room. Jim in the meantime had found an empty chair for me and I sat down.

Talk got around to vacation trips some of the people there had taken that summer.

Jim broke in. "You should hear Fred tell you about the trip he once took through the dust bowl in the Dakotas."

"Oh, it wasn't much, really," I said. "I was just hitchhiking through it."

"No, go on and tell them." Jim gave everybody a warm smile. "Fred really saw some pretty raw stuff."

I still demurred. I was quite aware that even when I told a dirty story I had trouble holding people's attention, especially if there were a lot of people around. Two people, maybe; more, no. I was still too ill-at-ease, too shy, in crowds. In college I'd had trouble reciting in large classes. Also, when I finally did get started, I had a tendency to tell too much, get sidetracked on some juicy detail.

"Go on. Tell about the hobo and the snake. And oh yes, especially about that old maid."

III

"Well, all right."

So I started at the beginning. Within a few minutes I noticed that everybody in Jim's living room had fallen silent. Encouraged, I began to go into more detail, to dramatize what had happened to me. Here and there I embroidered the tale some. When I finished there were wide smiles, a few belly laughs, and many questions.

Later, on the way home around two o'clock, having completely forgotten about looking for a girl at Jim's house, I was in a glow. For once in my life I'd finally told a story well enough to hold everybody's attention.

For months, ever since I'd started work on the *Journal* and had brought myself a portable typewriter, I'd also been trying to write stories. I'd read Hemingway for a while and then try to write like him. Result: an overly mannered Ernie. Then I'd read Steinbeck for a while and try to write like him. Result: an overly sentimental John. And then I'd read Dos Passos and try to write like him, especially Dos's poetic biographies of Veblen and La Follette and Hearst. Result: things that sounded like *Daily Worker* sob stories. Imitations, apings, all of them.

Sitting behind my steering wheel, it came to me what I should do: write the way I'd told that dust bowl story that night. Somehow I'd done something right there. I hadn't told the tale as a Hemingway might tell it, but had told it according to *the way I saw it in my head*. I wasn't seeing the tale through someone else's eyes or out of someone else's vision, but through my own eyes and out of my vision. With my kind of hesitations in it, and my way of breathing, and my way of talking. Even my way of walking behind the cows bringing them up from the pasture. Me. Therefore *my* style.

When I got to my room, instead of going to bed, I went directly to my typewriter, got out a wad of paper, and completely forgetting that earlier I'd been pooped,

IV

started in, retelling that tale of the Dirty Thirties. I knew that if I waited until morning the mood and the method would be gone.

I wrote through the rest of that night and all the next morning and well into the afternoon. As I went along, it delighted me to see my imagination go to work on that wonderful tour of the Dust Bowl. I filled some fifty plus pages.

Then I went down the street and had myself a lake trout dinner at the Bridge Cafe. And at last went to bed.

The next night after work, Monday evening, I got out the fifty plus pages and read them.

When I finished reading them, I slowly got up out of my chair and ran a hand through my hair. "You know," I said to myself, "by God, I can write. I've found out who I am as a writer. I've found my tone, my pacing, my angle of vision. This is the way I've got to do it. The hell with Hemingway and Steinbeck and Dos Passos."

In the next months I completely rewrote that first draft, singling out in particular the part having to do with the hobo and the snake and building it into a novel. That novel, after seven different tries at it, was later published in 1944 as *The Golden Bowl.*

What follows then in this book is the story, a reminiscence, I told that magic night at Jim's house. The reminiscence is written in the third person. The Frederick Feikema* of those days is forty-five years back there in time. He's enough of a stranger to me today to write about him as though he were a Hugh Glass. Also, by putting it in the third person, it helped me to see myself as others see me, as well as helped me dredge up from memory many facts and incidents I didn't get around to telling that night at Jim's house.

V

Thus do not be too startled when you see that the first name of the hero is also the first name of the writer.

Frederick Feikema Manfred
Spring, 1979
Roundwind RR3
Luverne, Minnesota 56156

*I added Manfred legally in 1952.

THE WIND BLOWS FREE

I

Fred drove the line of cows up the pasture lane and then into the barnyard. There was a heavy dew out and for once there was no dust underfoot. The sun was just up, and it deepened the red of the Shorthorn cows and the red of the old barn. It gave the white country house near the garden a touch of pink.

The grass in the night pasture across the fence wasn't quite dead. Here and there a green spear still stuck out. It'd been overgrazed and the turf had the look of a shaved cougar. The alfalfa field to the east of the lane also lay waiting; the stubble left over from the last cutting looked like old gray whiskers.

Pa appeared in the doorway of the cow barn. He leaned over the lower half of the door and watched the lead cow, Old Belle, come toward him. When the cows were within a dozen steps of him, Pa opened the lower door and stood to one side to let them come in. Instead, Old Belle and the dozen milk cows headed for the cement cattle tank. Their heavy udders swung back and forth, almost throwing them out of step. They crowded in and began sipping eagerly at the green water. Some of them had to lower their rubbery muzzles down between floating islands of mushy moss.

When the cows finished drinking, they swiveled around and headed for the open door. Solemnly they hocked up the cement approach and walked inside one by one. Each one went straight for her stanchion and her little mound of ground oats.

Pa looked at Fred's bare feet. "Ain't the ground hot?"

"Not yet." Fred smiled. "You take it too hard, Pa. There's a great smell down in the pasture this morning. Especially in the lower draw."

"Dew don't help roots much."

3

"When the sun comes up, it always makes me feel good." Fred looked at the light-blue sky above. When he stretched to his full height he stood a good five inches taller than Pa. "Really, it's a great morning, Pa."

"Hum."

"Coming up the pasture this morning I made up my mind."

Pa waited.

"I've got to see the mountains first before I take on any kind of job. Because once you take a job, the next thing you know you find yourself married. And then you never get to see the sights."

"You ain't seen enough of the world yet hitchhiking between here and college?"

"That kind of traveling don't count. I mean, I want to follow my toes around for a while. For the fun of it."

Pa scuffed at the dry ground. The wide pantleg of his Baker overalls hid his workshoe. "A hobo at heart, I see. Like your grampa, Old Feike. He had the wandering bug too."

"And you didn't have a wild hair when you were young?"

Pa thought to himself a moment. "I guess I did at that."

"There's no work around here for me, Pa."

"I know."

"I've got to see the Black Hills. And Yellowstone National Park. The Shining Mountains."

"And after you see them, then what?"

"Well, after I visit my old roommate, Don, up in Belgrade, Montana, come back home here, and then see again. Don, by the way, is starting Calvin Seminary this fall and I can probably ride back with him."

"Too bad you can't start the Seminary this fall yourself. That's something your Ma wanted."

4

"Me a minister? Never, Pa."

Pa took hold of the lower half of the door. He gestured for Fred to step inside ahead of him. "C'mon, time to pail them cows."

After breakfast Fred went upstairs to pack. He heard Pa assign jobs to his younger brothers Edward and Floyd, Edward to clean out the hog house and Floyd to get out the gang plow and start fall plowing. Plowing had always been Fred's job before. It was a job Fred loved. One worked alone with five horses far from the house and there was always plenty of time to dream about things while riding the plow.

Fred decided to travel light. He got out his beat-up leather suitcase and packed a pair of socks, several handkerchiefs, and only one extra set of underwear. Having heard it got cold nights in the Rockies, he folded in his college blanket. Playing on the basketball team in his senior year, he'd chosen a maroon wool blanket instead of the usual sweater with a letter. He already had two sweaters with a letter. The maroon blanket was trimmed in gold and had three gold stars and a gold emblem resembling a basketball sewn in one corner and his name *Fred Feikema* and the year 1934 in another corner.

After some thought he decided not to take along his pipe and tobacco, nor his cigarette makings. A couple of weeks earlier he'd quit smoking. Too expensive when he had so little money. And, it was dangerous in drouth times. The stubblefields and pastures were as dry as tinder.

Next he tucked in three books: the Bible, Shakespeare's *Works,* and Whitman's *Leaves of Grass.* He'd have something good to read in case he got stuck in a deserted place somewhere. The Bible he'd got from the Doon Christian Grammar School upon graduating

5

from the eighth grade, a black limp/leather gold-edged beauty of a book. Shakespeare's *Works* he'd bought from Sears Roebuck with money he'd earned picking corn his first year out of high school.

He especially liked *Leaves of Grass,* a big brown volume, with green lettering on its title page, bought just a month before in Grand Rapids, Michigan.

. . . . He was working with Deb on the campus at Calvin College when it finally hit him he was a fool to think he could ever win That Special Face over. He could perform all the heroic arts of a Hercules, but it still wouldn't do a bit of good. Oh, she might let him come visit her in her house but she'd still keep him at arm's length while singing "Smoke Gets in Your Eyes." A fool. Yes, dammit, he just simply had to forget her. Somehow.

So at eleven o'clock one morning, in the middle of July 1934, with the sun shining on the snowball bushes outside the Girl's Room in Old Main, he jabbed his spade in the dirt and turned to his buddy and said, "Deb, I've had enough. I'm going home to see Pa and then I'm going West and see the mountains."

Fred headed for the business office to settle his account with the college. Professor Dekker asked him how much money he had on him. Fred said he had one dollar. A strange look came over Professor Dekker's face and then he told the business manager to give Fred ten dollars. The ten raised Fred's debt at the college from seventy-nine to eighty-nine dollars.

Back at Butler Hall, his apartment, he stored his hundred or more books up in the attic; packed his suitcase; showered; and dressed in his burgundy pants and red slipover sweater. Then, just before hitting the road, he went downtown to The Bookery, an incense-sweet

6

bookstore in Grand Rapids, and bought *Leaves of Grass.* Price: $2.98. And with eight dollars and two cents in his pocket, walked out to the end of Division Avenue and caught a ride for Kalamazoo.

"The heck with Special Face. If she isn't big enough to ignore what her mother said about me, that I'm too big for her, that the thought of having a child with me was just too awful to contemplate . . . well, too bad for her" . . . .

Pa called up the stairwell. "Say, mister."
"Yes?"
"I have to go to town and get some store bread. Want a lift?"
"You bet."
"Better come then. Right now."

Fred hurried to finish packing. The last item he tucked in was his "word book," a narrow fat notebook. It was leatherbound, black, and a little more than half-filled with new words he'd collected from all his reading, along with a cryptic definition for each word. He called it his vocabulary builder. He'd started it the year before and found it helped his reading immensely. He now rarely ran into a word he didn't know the meaning of. He made it a point to use a couple of newly found words each day. Too often though the new words didn't quite fit. They sounded carpentered in, when a word should just pop out in one's talk naturally.

He checked his money. He'd earned a little money shocking grain for a neighbor but as it turned out he had almost exactly the same sum he had when leaving Grand Rapids, eight dollars and some loose change. He dropped the loose change in his pants pocket, slipped one dollar in his wallet, and put seven dollars in the bottom of his shoe.

7

When he got downstairs, he looked around for Hattie, his stepmother, and her girls, Irene and Jean.

"Ma's in the bedroom. She don't feel well." Pa was having his last sip of coffee. Pa was a coffee hound.

Fred nodded. That meant Hattie was mad at him again. He was taking off to see the world when what she wanted was for him to help Pa farm and so make money for the family.

"Want a last cup of coffee?"

"Don't mind if I do."

Pa poured him a cup and pushed the creamer and sugar toward him.

"Where are the kids?"

"They went plumming. That's about the only good crop around this year. The wild plums are wonderful."

Fred nodded. He wished he could have given them each a hug, Johnnie and Abben and Henry. Even Hattie's girls, Irene and Jean. And of course Floyd was in the field plowing and Ed was probably standing somewhere in the hog yard daydreaming to himself.

Pa stood up and stretched to his full height, six foot four. "Well, let's go." He clapped on his town hat.

Fred pushed his cup and saucer to the middle of the table. He stared a moment at the blue-checkered tablecloth that Ma'd bought just before she'd died and then got to his feet and followed Pa out the door.

Pa wheeled the old dark-blue Chevy up the lane. The lane led past the old white cypress water tower and then widened into the main street of Doon, Iowa. Pa let the old car idle down past the banker's red house in the Silk Stocking district, then past the tennis courts, and then the first of the stores. Pa said, "Wanna take a last look in the mailbox?"

"Yes. Pull up."

Fred checked Box 124. There was a letter in it ad-

8

dressed to him. From the handwriting, *Frederick Feikema,* he could tell it was from Aunt Kathryn, Pa's sister. Both Aunt Kathryn and Ma liked to call him Frederick. Instead of Fred or Fritz. Or Feike, the family petname for the oldest son of the oldest son. Fred himself preferred his full first name Frederick. Fred climbed back into the old Chevy.

Pa recognized the handwriting too. "Nah, ain't you gonna read it?"

"It can wait until later. You know how Aunt Kathryn is, so worried over my future."

Pa pursed up his lips, "Well, I wouldn't mind knowing if they're all right. She is my sister, you know."

"All right." Fred slit the letter open with his finger and read it aloud for Pa. Just as he thought. Aunt Kathryn wanted to know why he hadn't taken that job teaching in a Lyon County country school. That was how she got started. And he had to start somewhere, didn't he? "One can't be too choosey in the beginning, you know. Great things come from humble beginnings. Don't be too proud." Aunt Kathryn also mentioned she and Uncle Clarence were in excellent health, as good as could be expected.

Pa sat a moment in thought. Then all of a sudden he slapped the steering wheel. "What a difference, what a difference."

Fred looked at him questioningly.

"Why can't she bake bread like Alice did? Why must my kids eat store-bought bread? My kids are beginning to look poorly. While hers are getting fat on it, sitting around like they do."

Fred said nothing. Hattie didn't like to bake. While Ma had enjoyed making great meals for her growing boys.

Pa started to cry. "I married me a wild one, I guess."

9

Fred blinked. Fred wasn't too wild about Hattie, but calling her wild, that was going a little too far. "C'mon now, Pa. She likes you. And her girls love you."

"Alice didn't care much for it, but this woman . . . heh."

Fred recalled the last talk he'd had with Ma. She'd warned him that should he get married someday he must remember that the woman didn't enjoy sex as much as the man did.

After a few moments, Pa caught himself. He straightened up immediately. "Well, where shall I drop you off?"

"North of town there. Where 18 used to split away from 75."

Pa cocked his head. "In the real old days we'd have said, where the Atlantic-Yellowstone-Pacific Highway used to split away from the King's Trail."

Pa cruised to the end of Main Street and then headed north past Miller's sandpit. He pulled up at the corner where Nellie Brower used to live. Nellie graduated with Fred from the Doon Christian Grammar School. He'd been a little sweet on her once, even though she'd been fifteen to his twelve. She'd had brown eyes and wonderful legs. By the time he graduated from high school she'd married a barber and disappeared.

Pa pulled up. "You sure you have to do this?"

"Pa, I've got to see the mountains."

"If that's your mind."

Fred got out with his suitcase. Fred was so happy to be heading out on a new and wonderful adventure that for once he didn't have that old stricture in his chest when bidding Pa good-bye. "So long, Pa."

Pa saluted him, and then, holding his face away from him, lurched off in his dark-blue Chevy.

Fred didn't have long to wait. A truck loomed up out of town. It was Walt, the local trucker. He was an older brother of Irene Levering. Besides Nellie Brower, Fred had also been sweet on Irene. Irene's silver hair had the sheen of the undersides of maple leaves. Walt had a shy smile. Pa'd often said of Walt that if he'd had gumption he'd have made a great southpaw pitcher.

Walt pulled up with iron-whining brakes. "Going somewhere?"

"Well, first to Sioux Falls."

"Hop in."

Fred climbed in. "I see you're riding empty."

"Yeh." Walt gunned the motor, and started rolling again. "Just had a call from the stockyards in Sioux Falls that they had some cattle to haul east. Buzzard bait. Too thin to butcher."

"What'll they do with them east?"

"Some cattle feeder near Spirit Lake is taking 'em on. They had rain out there."

"Does the original owner get anything for them?"

"He gets paid for whatever they weigh when we pick them up. And the new owner gets paid for the weight he adds."

The truck rolled across the Big Rock River bridge. The river was dried up. Only the deeper holes had a little green water in them. Rotting carp lay in the shallower holes.

At the next corner Walt took a left for Inwood. They bumped across rich bottom land but even there the corn had begun to die from the ground up. The tassel still had a fresh gold color and the top leaves were green, but the ears had turned yellow. Walt gestured with his head.

"That feller might just be lucky to get nubbins out of that."

Fred nodded. He was still thinking about Pa's outburst back in Doon. What a terrible thing it was that Ma had to die. When Ma was alive they'd had a happy family. Fred could remember only two fights between Pa and Ma, and they were hardly more than spats. But now with this Hattie, Pa's second wife, there was nothing but pouting lips and black brows and occasional flying pans.

They ground up a slight rise. Here the country was even drier, especially over the low yellow hills. Almost all the cornfields looked as though they'd had a severe killing frost in midsummer.

Walt said, "Even the birds are leaving."

"Nothing for them to eat."

"And I bet the night animals are leaving too. Coons and skunks."

Fred slid down in the seat a little. "Saw a funny thing on the lawn the other day. You know how a robin will take a couple of steps and listen, take a couple more steps and listen again, and then suddenly peck down and come up with the tail of a worm in its beak? Well, this robin worked our whole lawn, taking a couple of steps and listening, over and over, but not once did he hear a worm sliding in the ground."

The tower of Inwood appeared over a hill. Then town itself came into view. The ash trees were having a tough time of it. A good third of them had lost the battle. And the lawns were like those back in Doon, so dry they looked like denuded fur robes.

The Inwood road connected with the new 18. It had been freshly graveled. Dust stived up behind them in pale clouds.

The land began to break off into gullies and deep

12

ravines. The road hooked onto the right shoulder of the deepest ravine and then curved down toward the valley. Abruptly below lay the trees along the Big Sioux River, and a mile beyond it the glinting roofs of Canton, South Dakota. Here the trees were different. They were tough scrub oak and they'd survived the drouth in fairly good shape. Only an occasional inner leaf hung sere and brown.

Fred spotted the academy where Ole Rölvaag had gone to school. His own high school, Western Academy in Hull, had sometimes played Augustana Academy in basketball and had battled their debate teams. The grounds around Rölvaag's old school were spacious with a fine view toward the bluffs across the river.

Fred hardly noted downtown Canton going by. He'd fallen into a reverie in which, somehow, he and Ole Rölvaag were locked in a rip-rousing debate on the question of whether or not Siouxland should ever have been broken with a plow. Fred argued that Siouxland should have been set aside for ranching. Therefore Per Hansa, for all his being a hero, was actually an instrument of destruction. Ole had a pretty good comeback. "My honorable opponent, Frederick Feikema, has a point all right, except that he is referring to the wrong hero. The man he is actually thinking of is not my Per Hansa, but his own grandfather, Feike Feikes Feikema V, who tried to farm in what is now known as The Badlands. One look and he should have known it was folly to plow there." Fred was scratching around in his head for a scorching rebuttal, when he was interrupted. Walt Levering beside him had asked him something.

"What?"

"I say, after Sioux Falls, then what?"

"I'm gonna see the mountains."

"You gonna catch rides all the way?"

13

"I hope to."

"Not many people traveling these days."

"Salesmen are still making their runs."

Walt allowed himself a gentle smile. "Yeh, them and the insurance investigators. They've got plenty of money to travel, repossessing all that land from poor farmers."

Fred nodded. Pa and Uncle Henry also had strong things to say about insurance people.

Walt took the shortcut off 18 onto 77. The wind had come up, and light veils of dust lifted out of the plowed fields and moved across the road. Some of the roadside ditches were partially filled with dust. The dust drifts had the ribbed look of snowbanks. No wonder people in the area spoke of the dust storm of a week ago as a black blizzard. A strong wind had started up at midnight, and by morning there'd been so much dust in the air the sun didn't come up. People stayed inside all day. Dinner at noon was eated by lamp light. Pa instructed everybody to wear a wetted handkerchief over his mouth and nose. When they'd separated milk that night, the cream had come out of the spout like rusty blood.

"What do you want to see the mountains for?"

Fred wrinkled his nose at the sharp smell of burning oil rising off the engine. "I've heard about 'em so much that I've just simply got to see 'em."

"From them books you're always reading?"

"Yes, And then I had a college buddy who came from the mountains."

"Them cowboy stories you was always reading as a kid, you know of course that that's a lot of horseshit. Not even good manure."

Fred threw Walt a look. It surprised him that gentle Walt should use rough language. Fred decided to say nothing. Except for the doctor in Doon, there was no one around he could talk to.

14

They crested a bluff. Below lay the looping Big Sioux River again, and beyond it the pink towers of Sioux Falls. A good share of the downtown buildings were made of local pink quartzite, and even at noon, when there were no shadows to highlight things, Sioux Falls had the magic air of a holy city. With its curling river and all its trees it was a fabled oasis on the flat plains, where down one of its streets one might have a lot of fun for a little while.

"Hungry?"

"No." Fred knew Walt was having a hard time making ends meet and didn't want to sponge off him. "Not really. It's still only eleven o'clock."

"Where do you want to be dropped off?"

"Where 77 crosses 16."

They rolled under high umbrella elms. The houses on the outskirts of town had a scabby look about them, but the homes nearer downtown still had good paint. It was a relief to be riding on paved streets — no dust, no washboards to shake a car apart.

Fred spotted a tall willowy girl slowly dreaming down a sidewalk by herself. She walked as if she'd just finished a long hard run and was enjoying the luxury of just loafing along. She had long blond hair, falling in a gold drift over her shoulders, and the thinnest waist he'd ever seen. There was a hint of abandon in each lagging step she took. Now there was one for him. But before he could do anything about it, ask Walt to stop, the truck turned a corner and she was gone.

Walt pulled up near the YMCA. "Here you are."

Fred reached for his suitcase up on the shelf behind the seat and stepped down. "Thanks a lot for the lift."

"Don't mention it. And don't do anything I wouldn't do."

"Why, Walt, what could that be?"

"You might be surprised." Walt showed mink teeth. "I ain't all that slow."

Fred laughed. It was probably true. "Take it easy, Walt."

"And a pantsful to you too, sir." Walt waved, and eased out the clutch, and was off. The old truck listed slightly to the right as it took the corner past The Palace of Sweets.

Fred watched Walt go with regret. Walt had a soul of sweet silver. There were all too few of his kind. It would have been very nice to have been related to him.

III

Fred walked over to a Standard Oil station down the street.

An old gentleman with brush-stiff gray hair and freshly ironed blue trousers was sitting inside with feet up on a battered desk. The place was oily neat.

The old gentleman gave Fred a sour look. "Another bum looking for a handout, I see."

Fred quick checked his own clothes. His burgundy trousers hung in a straight crease all the way to his tan oxfords. His red tie was still snugged up neat into his shirt collar. Fred smiled. "I see you got out of bed on the wrong side this morning."

"What do you want?"

"I could use a couple of maps. South Dakota. Wyoming."

"Do you drink gas?"

"Homebrew beer, yes. Gas, no."

"Then you can't have any."

"Suppose I bought a candy bar?"

The old gentleman swung his feet down and popped upright out of his swivel chair. Four quick strides and he was standing behind an open candy case. "What would you like? O'Henry? Baby Ruth?"

It made Fred smile some more. He set down his suitcase and ambled over. The O'Henry was bigger than the Baby Ruth. "I think I'll take the short story over the homerun."

"Come again?" The old gentleman's hair ridged up under his blue attendant's cap. "You threw me a curve there, son, when I'm a fastball hitter."

"You played ball?"

"With the old Sioux Falls Canaries."

"Hey, I always wanted to pitch against them."

"Who'd you pitch for?" the old gentleman asked.

"Doon."

"I've heard about 'em. Got a long-legged kid pitchin' there . . . Naw. That can't be you, can it?"

"Your guess is as good as mine."

"Hell. Take all the maps you want."

Fred asked, "What did you play?"

"Shortstop."

"Then you were part of that doubleplay combination with Swede Risberg."

"The same. And was he good."

Risberg had been kicked out of the American League for throwing games while playing for the White Sox in a World Series with the Cincinnati Reds. Fred was curious to know what Risberg was like in real life but decided the old gentleman might not like to talk about Risberg's shady past. There'd been some talk that Swede Risberg had too many friends in the underworld of Chicago. "I better have a candy bar anyway. For later on when I'm down the road a ways. I'll take the O'Henry."

The old gentleman handed him the candy bar. "What was that about taking the short story over the homerun?"

Fred dug a nickel out of his collection of loose change and handed it over. "A fellow named O'Henry wrote short stories."

"I didn't know that."

Fred stepped over to the Standard Oil map rack and took a map for both South Dakota and Wyoming. Both covers showed a pair of gray geese winging their way across a deep blue sky with a red car below zooming along a blue road. Both goose and car were headed east, not west. The land was shown in purple with a white halo along the horizon. "Thanks."

18

"Don't mention it. And the next time you throw me an O'Henry curve, telegraph it a little, will you? I'm only a .241 hitter."

Fred laughed. "Them I always had the most trouble with."

Out on the street again, Fred looked east up 16. No cars in sight. After a little thought, Fred decided he'd better walk out to the west end of town. There he'd be sure to catch any Sioux Falls traffic heading west.

He walked under more huge elms. Some of the underbranches were dead. The lawns and porches were mostly neat.

Fred kept glancing over his shoulder on the watch for rides. A drayman came by. Too short a ride. A block farther along a jitney full of yelling young toughs, all of high school age, roared by, cutout open. "Hey, long gears, how's the weather up there?"

"Why don't you grow up and find out?" Fred yelled back with a smile.

Highway 16 jogged left several blocks, then speared straight west. The houses slowly turned drab and the lawns became more littered.

A freshly painted combination filling station and cafe glinted near the last stoplight. Two trucks waited to one side of it. The drivers were inside having a cup of coffee. A good place to hook rides. Fred set down his suitcase. He checked his necktie and fly and got out his smile. He was ready.

Across the street stood the last house. The lawn around it had been watered just enough to keep it a fresh green. It was almost an eyesore it was so lovely. Looking closer, Fred spotted a private well. The fellow had been lucky enough to hit a good vein of water.

The sun was almost overhead. Fine particles of dust riding very high gave the atmosphere a strange platinum sheen. Close up, though, the air appeared to be clear.

Two cars came down the pike. Fred warmed up his smile and stuck out his thumb. Fred had worked out a pretty good rule of thumb about hitchhiking. Salesmen, of course, were the best to flag for a ride. They usually liked company and often asked a hiker to drive for them while they took a snooze between calls. Their cars were also the best. Occasionally they even fed a guy after a long run. Next came the singleton tourist driving through to the West Coast. He was easily spotted. He generally had an eastern license plate and the back seat piled full of suitcases. Farmers were no good; they were only going a few miles and always dropped one off at a lonely corner where the traffic was going by full blast. No one cared to stop when going at top speed. Old hens, of course, never stopped for strangers. They right away thought of rape and speeded up in a cloud of dust. And young girls rarely traveled alone. Too bad.

The first car turned out to be a hearse. Well, that was one way to get to the holy city in a hurry. The other car was full up. No room for a hitchhiker and his suitcase.

To the west the horizon had a bronze cast. It glimmered a little. High and far out the sky of another world spread endlessly off into the distance.

Fred noticed some activity near some lilac bushes on the far side of the last house. It was a boy and a dog. The dog was digging a hole, furiously, in spurts, in various directions. Between each spurt the dog shoved his nose down into the hole and sniffed, quick, sharp, and then with a snort started digging again. The dog was a mongrel, a mixture of a shepherd and a rat terrier, browns and blacks, with a white throat. The boy had to keep dodging the flying dirt as the dog worked on different angles at the hole. Dig, dig. Sniff. Snort. Dig, dig.

20

Fred's eyes moistened in memory. When he'd been a little boy he too had watched his dog Rover dig for gophers. Once, when Rover'd got tired, and had lain down to puff, Fred'd picked up a couple of little sticks, one in each hand, and had helped Rover with the hole. He'd dug, dug, like Rover; then also like Rover had stuck his nose down into the dark hole, which got darker the deeper he nosed into it, and had sniffed for all he was worth. And had smelled the gopher. It was the way Eddie his brother smelled when he was afraid he was going to get a licking. He and Rover had dug after that gopher one whole afternoon, and then, just before suppertime, Rover got it. He caught hold of its tail and jerked it out. The gopher tried to gallop off the end of its tail. Rover regrabbed the gopher with his mouth, and then with a growl at little Freddie to stay away, settled in the grass and ate it. Later when Pa came along, he cussed something fierce at the way Rover and Freddie had torn up the pasture. "By God," Pa told Ma, "those two are worse than a pair of badgers. Why, that part of the pasture looks like a battlefield."

Fred watched the boy and the dog. It didn't surprise him, after a while, to see the boy take over the digging when the dog lay on its belly to rest. Only the boy didn't use a pair of sticks like he had. The boy dug with his fingernails. Dirt flew out between his legs. And the boy also stuck his nose down into the dark hole for a long deep sniff. Then, backing out, the boy barked in frustration exactly like the dog.

Fred laughed outloud. The boy was more of a dog than the dog was.

The stoplight in the middle of the highway clicked from red to yellow to green.

A cattle truck with a South Dakota license plate pulled up in the combination filling station and cafe.

21

Instead of cattle it was full of people. A dozen of them. They stared out with glazed eyes.

The driver and another man got out of the truck's red cab and entered the cafe. They didn't look back at the load of people up in the rack.

The stoplight in the middle of the road clicked from green to yellow to red.

Presently the driver and his friend came out picking their teeth. They strolled along in an easy loafing manner. The friend got in on his side of the red cab and the driver came around on the near side kicking rubber and then climbed in.

Fred bet the truck was going a long ways.

The driver caught Fred's look. He fiddled with the knob on the shift. He looked back through the rear window at the people behind him and then looked back at Fred.

Fred picked up his suitcase and stepped over. "Got room for one more?"

The driver smiled easy. He was heavily freckled. His cap was tipped back and his forehead was so sunburned the skin had begun to scale off. "Steer or bull?"

"How about a maphrodite?"

"Can't start up a new country with them."

"Oh, I dunno now. Plato thought so."

"You mean, in Plato, South Dakota, they do?"

Fred laughed. "No. How far you going?"

"I turn off at Kennebec."

"Say, that's quite a ways."

"West River Country."

"Can I?"

"At your service." The driver noticed Fred's neat clothes. "Just take it easy leaning against the rack. I took some cattle out east first to greener pastures before I picked up these people on the way back."

22

Fred nodded.

"What was that about Plato again?"

"Oh, a guy named Plato once wrote about a race of people who had two faces and a double set of arms and legs." Fred had loved being a member of the Plato Club back in Calvin College. He'd gotten more out of that club than he had out of any class. "Round and fat like an apple dumpling."

The driver let go with a good laugh. He had a two-day growth of red beard and his eyes and teeth flashed white. "That's them guys from Plato all right. Round and fat. And about as two-faced as you can get."

Fred went around in back, and setting his suitcase inside, leaped aboard. The first step he took he almost slipped and fell. The trucker had thrown some straw on the floor of the truck to cover fresh cow dung and Fred had the tough luck of stepping where a fresh pile of it lay hidden. Fred quick steadied himself by grabbing a sideboard.

The driver hit the starter and after a second muffled explosions shook the truck. There was a smooth meshing of gears expertly done and with an easy lurch they were off.

Before the wind got too strong Fred quick had a peek at his South Dakota map. Kennebec. Kennebec. There it was, some forty miles beyond the Missouri River. By nightfall he should be halfway to the Black Hills.

When he looked around for a clean spot along the rack sideboards he found that all the good places were taken. He'd have to ride standing up, knees slightly bent, balancing himself, ready for any roll of the truck. He placed his suitcase between his feet.

There were exactly a dozen people aboard. A family of five, father, mother, three young boys, had the best place. They were lined up against the back of the red

23

cab. They wore wash-faded clothes. Five grain hands stood along the right side of the truck rack, each with a well-beaten duffel bag. It was always easy to spot a grain hand working his way north with the ripening wheat. He invariably carried a pair of pliers in the plier pocket on the right trouser leg, a can of tobacco in the left rear pocket, makin's in the bib pocket, and a big red bandanna round his neck. His duffel bag was usually packed tight with an extra set of underwear, a half-dozen pair of extra brown work socks, handkerchiefs, and a fresh set of overalls and shirt for Saturday nights. A young couple stood on the left side of the rack. The two had apparently got on last; their side was the most crapped on. Going east, the cattle had stood facing the wind out of the south and had crapped north.

The couple looked at Fred with interest, a wondering smile on their lips. The man appeared to be about thirty, dark-skinned with curly black hair, wise crinkles at the corners of his black eyes, with the air of an actor. He wore New York-cut clothes, blue jacket and blue trousers, light-blue shirt open at the collar, and two-tone shoes. The girl was much younger, about twenty, a vivid gold blond with very light-blue eyes. She wore a rather tight yellow dress, quite short for the day, revealing a pair of marvelous legs. It was even more obvious she was an actress and more than likely one who would lap up flattery.

The truck hit a deep dip in the road and Fred almost lost his balance. He had to throw out his arms to keep from falling.

"Whoops," the girl said.

"Yeh," Fred said, turning pink.

The man shook his head in sympathy.

Fred took another look at the dung-spattered south side of the truck rack, finally decided he'd try a spot to the right of the couple where it was relatively free of cow manure. He shagged his suitcase over between his legs. Luckily the straw underfoot was free of suspicious-looking mounds. Gingerly Fred caught hold of one of the rack uprights.

The couple on his left rode the dips and swoops in the road with an easy grace. They were probably used to standing up in streetcars and subways. Fred envied them. He longed to see New York and its shimmering skyscrapers someday.

Exhaust fumes from the truck mingled with the smell of urine-soaked straw.

The couple watched the countryside go by with lively interest. They kept pointing things out to each other: a windmill beside a water tank, a red barn with white trim, a binder standing idle at the end of a field, cows and horses scattered across a pasture, chickens working the roadside ditches. They had the air of visitors at a zoo.

The truck picked up speed and the wind got worse. Because Fred stuck out a good foot above everybody he really got a blasting. His ears boomed with it sometimes. Fred liked to go bareheaded but the way the wind was whipping his hair around, sometimes in his eyes so that it was like looking through a brown veil, he wondered if maybe he shouldn't dig out his blue cap from his suitcase.

The red truck bumped on the pavement cracks one after another. Heads bobbed on loose necks.

The road speared straight west, its gray cement slowly turning white in the distance until it finally vanished into what looked like a little hole. The bronze haze along the horizon began to deepen.

"It's all so flat," the girl said to Fred.

In the bruising wind Fred wasn't sure he'd caught

25

what she'd said. "Flat? Wait a while. This country is full of surprises."

"Never having seen anything like it before, I find it all fascinating."

The fellow beside her slipped his arm around her. "What I don't understand is how people can make a living here." The fellow had a sauve mellow voice. "I mean, what do people do during drought times?"

Fred laughed. "I wonder about the same thing when I ride past all those endless blocks of houses in Chicago."

"I don't get you."

"Well, what can they be doing for work when they aren't raising some kind of produce? Who pays them for doing what?"

It was the fellow's turn to laugh. "Yes, I guess it's all in how you look at it, all right." He glanced at Fred's tie. "I'm Sam Rivers. And this is my wife Joan."

"Glad to meet you. And I'm" — Fred held up a label on one side of his red college sweater on which his name had been sewn — "I'm Frederick Feikema. See?" With strangers Fred was always hesitant to give his last name. People rarely caught it right the first time and almost always mispronounced it. Pronunciations ranged all the way from Fee-ke-ma, with the accent on either the first or second syllable, to Frycake, with a sneer in the voice. It hurt to hear one's family name mangled. There were even several dirty variations, and that really got him. But it helped if the stranger could see the name in print.

Rivers gave the name a second glance. "Feikema. What nationality is that?"

"Frisian."

Rivers' dark eyes lit up. "Oh yes. I've run into that in my dictionary. The Frisians were related to the Angles

26

and Saxons and once helped settle England."

Fred began to feel better about the couple.

"Do you speak Frisian?"

"I heard it around me as a boy. My father and his uncles. So I understand most of it. In fact, when I went to college I was surprised to learn I could read Chaucer."

"Holy mud."

"I wasn't just a member of a minority group within a minority group. A stiff-necked Frisian despised by a dumb Dutchman who in turn was laughed at by Americans. But about as English as one could be. Old English even. Suddenly I was a charter member of the English-speaking world."

Rivers' eye fell on the single gold stripe on the left arm of Fred's sweater. "I bet you played center."

"Yeh."

"I bet you could just reach up and drop 'em in."

Joan looked up at Fred's height and then glanced down at the front of his trousers. She slipped her arm around Rivers.

Rivers said, "You from around here?"

"Just left my home town Doon about an hour ago. Back over in Iowa there."

"How come you're riding west instead of east?"

"I'm out to see the mountains. I've already seen the east a little. Lived four years in Grand Rapids where I went to college."

"But you haven't seen New York?"

"Nope."

"That's the place to go."

"That's where you're from, aren't you? You both look like actors."

Rivers and Joan glanced at each other. "What makes you say that?"

"You both look like you've been sanded off a little."

27

Rivers crooked his head to one side. "I'll be damned. But you're right, Frederick. I was an actor. But now I'm a writer. I just had a play of mine put on in an off-Broadway theatre. It ran for about two months, and made me some money, and when it closed down, we decided to see the country." Rivers gave his wife a little pull against his side. "Joan here had one of the lead roles in it."

Fred narrowed his eyes at Rivers. A playwright. Fred wondered if he dare tell Rivers that he wanted to be a writer too someday.

The driver let up on the footfeed, and the truck began to coast. Ahead was a crossroad. Junction 19. A sign read: *Pumpkin Center.* But there was no town. Only a filling station and a leanto cafe on the north side of the road.

Inside the cab the driver and the rider were talking. Then with the truck still moving, the rider stepped out on the running board and called back, "Anybody need to stop here?"

Everyone looked at everyone else; shook their heads.

The rider slid back into his seat and closed the door after himself. The trucker stepped on the gas.

"Where are the pumpkins?" Rivers wanted to know.

Fred shrugged. "Probably raised a lot of pumpkins around here once."

They rolled on mile after mile. Bump-a-bump-a-bump. The thudding tires and the creaking side of the rack worked into bones and brains. The sun burned straight down.

Joan pointed ahead.

Fred craned his head to look past the edge of the rack. Ahead a valley opened, and in a moment the red truck began to drop into it. The driver let up on the footfeed and the engine fell to a murmur. Only the gears, dragging, ground a little. The valley turned out to be an enchanting sight. A little stream meandered down the center of it. Willows and cottonwoods with shiny leaves grew along its banks. A herd of cattle and some dozen horses cropped grass in a narrow meadow. One horse, a gray stallion, looked up at the rolling truck. The truck dropped, down and down; it was like taking a deep dip in a rollercoaster.

Rivers whispered, "Lovely."

Fred said, "Yes, just when you're about to give up on this country, it always comes through with a surprise. A little green valley."

"Look," Joan said. "What's that gray horse got under him there?"

"That's what's known as an erection," Rivers said.

"Is that what it is," Joan said. "Great. Now I've seen that."

Fred played it with a straight face. "Kind of a misnomer though to call that an erection when it's aimed down, not up, wouldn't you say?"

Rivers had to laugh.

"You!" Joan said.

The wheels of the red truck drummed over a wooden bridge. A sign read: *East Fork, Vermillion River.*

Joan continued to examine the stallion. "Kind of wierd. Like a rolling pin."

Again Rivers had to laugh. "More like the handle of a tennis racket."

As the truck rolled up the hill the engine took hold again. Gears ground. When the driver had to shift to second, the gears began to howl and the engine kicked out a little cloud of smoke. The driver shifted to low. The engine began to pound.

Joan tugged at her ear. Presently she picked a hairpin out of the bun in her hair and very carefully pried the

curved end of it around in her earhole. She gingerly lifted out a ball of wax the size of a pea.

Up on the table land once more the country again turned sere and dry. Corn stood half-burnt, not having quite eared out. There'd been some grain, but it was so short the farmer'd had to cut it with a mower instead of a binder.

Pastures resembled badly worn rugs.

Tumbleweeds hung caught in the fences. Sometimes they were piled so high the four barbwire strands looked more like thick hedges than fences.

Some of the farmers had plowed their stubblefields. The raw earth lay a pulverized light brown with no hint of moisture. Here and there in it were hard slick chunks of earth resembling well-troweled cement blocks.

Rivers pointed at the roadside ditch. "Isn't that blowing dust?"

Fred nodded. The wind was just strong enough to pick up the loose dust from the plowed field and carry it into the ditch. New dust banks were slowly forming across the ditch.

The truck picked up speed. The regular cracks in the cement paving clicked faster and faster. Bellies hardened against it. Kidneys hurt after a time.

Hard wind tugged at Fred's hair. It kept making new partings, first on the left, then on the right.

The sun moved directly overhead. Back home Pa and family would be eating a big dinner. Fred wet his lips several times, discovered they were coated with a thin film of finest dust, acrid and slightly salty. Alkaline.

Joan licked her lips too, revealing a fleshy tongue.

"We could all do with a drink of water," Fred said.

Rivers said, "We probably should have stopped back there and had us all a drink at that stream."

Fred hooked a finger over his nose. "Come to think of

31

it, it's a miracle it had running water. Back home the river's stopped running. Just a series of scummy pools."

They watched the barren farms pass by. The bronze cloud along the far west horizon slowly rose.

Fred worried about that bronze cloud. If it was a dust storm they were in for hell riding up on that open truck.

The woman sitting with her back against the red cab opened a voluminous gunny sack and came up with a thick paper bag. She peered into it, and then deftly began to pluck out some sandwiches. She handed one each to her three little boys, one to her husband, and last took one herself. She closed the paper bag. She did it all without apology. It was a duty and needed no explanation. The husband, however, threw a look at the others on the truck, especially at the five grain hands, as if to say he was sorry he couldn't share his bread with them. All five of the family ate slowly, thoroughly, as though they'd got used to making sure they got every last bit of nutrition out of their food.

Fred remembered the candy bar he'd bought. Like the husband he wasn't sure it was good manners to be eating when others couldn't. After jouncing along another mile, Fred finally couldn't resist stealthily sliding his hand into his pocket and teasing open one end of the candy bar. He broke off a chunk, and when the truck hit a particularly sharp bump, making everybody grab for support, he quick slid the chunk into his cheek. It didn't take long for the chunk of chocolate and nuts and caramel to melt and disappear.

Joan saw him swallow. She looked down at his pocket. "Taste good?"

Fred reddened. Peripheral vision was hard to beat. With a self-conscious smile he pulled out the rest of the candy bar and offered both Joan and Rivers each a bite.

Both smiled, and declined.

32

Out of the corner of his eye Fred could feel the five grain hands eying his candy bar too. One of them licked his lips. After a moment Fred decided it would be ridiculous to offer all five a bite from just one candy bar. It'd be better to put it away for later. He quietly folded over the open end and dropped the candy bar back into his pocket. The one bite he'd taken would have to be enough until the truck stopped somewhere up the line.

Again the flat table land dropped over into a little surprise valley. The sign by the little bridge read: *West Fork, Vermillion River.* But the West Fork was dry; not even scattered pools of water in the sharper deep turns. There were no trees. Only a few patches of buckbrush. And no cattle or horses. The narrow meadow on both sides of the stream had long ago been grazed off close to the ground.

Stanley Corners came up, where 81 crossed 16. There were two filling stations, one Standard and one Shell, and a general grocery store with a post office. Tumbleweeds were caught in the fence surrounding three setback houses. Someone had forgotten to hook the door to one of the privies and it whanged, whanged. It was as though someone inside the privy was vainly trying to kick it closed against the slowly pushing south wind.

The trucker slowed to second gear as the truck jerked across 81; then picked up speed again.

The bronze cloud in the west continued to rise in the sky. It slowly turned lighter in color.

Five miles more and Bridgewater came up with its cylinder-shaped water tower, black and glossy in the sunlight. There were some fifty homes and a main street two blocks long. It had trees but most were dead. The curbs along the west side of every street were fringed with dust drifts, all the result of black blizzards earlier in

33

the year. Here and there a tumbleweed bounced down the north-south avenues. There wasn't a building that didn't need paint.

The road crossed a railroad track and abruptly became a gravel road. The difference was dramatic. The road was mostly a series of ribbed bumps, worse than a washboard. Everybody up in the truck got an awful shaking. A fellow had to either close his mouth, teeth tight, or let his jaw hang loose. The breasts of the two women, the mother sitting against the red cab and Joan Rivers, jiggled as though the two women were caught up in beaters of a threshing machine. Dust stived up behind the truck. Sometimes the dust whirled back up into the truck.

Dead trees at the ends of pastures were stunted. Dwarfs. The plowed earth changed color, brown and gray and ochreous yellow.

The truck slipped down into yet another valley, this time a shallow one. The sign on the small bridge read: *Wolf Creek.*

The highway turned north. Immediately the dust behind the truck, pushed by the south wind, caught up with them and made everybody cough.

In the distance hung a black water tower.

Fred dug out his map of South Dakota. "That has to be Emery."

"Another little town," Joan said. "Och! They all look so awfully lonesome. It must be dreadful to live in them. So forsaken."

Fred put away his map. "Depends. It's all there if you know how to look for it. Births. Loves. Deaths. Myself, I kind of like little towns."

Rivers said, "But how can anyone be inspired to write in them? No theatre, no symphonies."

Fred licked dust off his lips. "Well now, take Emery

34

coming up here. It used to be a great place for music."

"Oh come now."

"Really. Where I went to high school, Hull, Iowa, they had a glee club and everybody went to hear it."

From Emery the road zigzagged west, then north, to Alexandria. The gravel highway gradually narrowed. Meeting oncoming cars the truck had to take to the shoulder of the road. The ditches were filled level with fine drifted dust and sometimes the wheels on the right side slewed as though caught in syrup.

The road got rougher; the yellow dust thicker. Everybody rode with lips closed tight. It was hard to daydream.

Fred kept picking up different scents as they rumbled along. Dry rot in fence posts. Sun-roasted buffalo grass. Crushed sunflowers. Cracked meadows. He could smell the too early fall of a late dry spring.

The road veered west. The sun rode over the red cab at three o'clock high. It burned into the eyes. The land was utterly flat with the horizons slightly curled up at the edges.

They passed one abandoned farm after another. The doors to the houses and the barns hung open, some of them on one hinge. Windmills clanged aimlessly. The horseballs in the barnyards were old and the manure piles by the hog houses resembled doormats.

The land tipped down and ahead lay a valley several miles wide. A river wriggled down the center of it fringed with trees. For once most of the trees had a few green leaves. A sign on a black suspension bridge read: *James River.* The river was still running, narrow trickles connecting stagnant opalescent pools. To either side of the trickles lay a cracked earth. Some of the cracks were several inches wide, forming a multitude of irregularly shaped clay cakes. Dead fish, carp and minnow, lay

35

bleaching on the hard clay cakes.

Across the river on the next rise a mile away loomed a silver water tower and the considerable spread of a little city.

"That's got to be Mitchell." Fred consulted his map. "Yep. The Corn Palace town."

"Corn? Palace?" Joan said.

"Every fall they cover a frame building with ears of corn. About three thousands bushels worth."

Rivers gave him a sliding smile. "I suppose with turrets and towers."

"Sure. They have a six-day festival every fall and everybody for miles around comes to town. Whites. Indians. Grain hands passing through."

"Did you ever go to one?"

"No. Heard about it though on the Yankton radio." Fred pursed his lips. "This fall there won't be much to celebrate. The birds'll have eaten much of the corn up on those walls."

It was hard talking and they fell silent again. The road became smoother beyond the bridge. A maintenance man had just passed through with a road grader.

The truck lifted up with the road into Mitchell. The houses on the edges of town were as sandblasted as those of the towns they had passed through. Most of the city lay to the north, and there the houses, sheltered by trees, had a better look about them. The paint on them was still in good shape.

They rolled into a truck stop. The driver pulled beside a gas tank, brakes squeaking. The motor, relieved of its load, murmured quietly; then, the key being turned, whuskered off into silence.

The driver got out. He looked up at the riders in the truck rack with a cracked smile. He stretched his arms and rose on his toes several times. "Time for coffee and

cream for the engine and gas and oil for the stomach."
He looked at Fred, and then at Rivers and Joan. "Privies
are around in back there."

"Thanks."

Everybody got down. The two women headed for the
door marked Women and the father and the three boys
headed for the door marked Men. The five grain hands
headed for the cafe for something to eat.

Fred found himself lingering behind with Rivers.
Fred had to go too but thought he'd wait until everybody
had finished.

Rivers shivered. "Lord, have I got high water."

Fred eased into a smile. "Well, maybe we should turn
you loose on the landscape. Relieve the drought."

"Yeah. Uhh." Rivers shivered again and slid a hand
into a pocket to pinch himself back.

"Like Pantagruel flushing out the streets of Paris."

"You've read Rabelais then."

"In college. Laughed my head off for weeks."

Rivers looked up at Fred with a quirked serious expression. "You like books."

"Yes."

"What's your ambition?"

"They tried to make a teacher out of me, but I didn't
like it. Then I thought a little about baseball, but I hurt
my arm when I was seventeen. Pitched three games in
two days. While also pitching bundles."

"You'd probably make a good first baseman."

"I thought about that too. And I can hit. But . . ."

"Yes?"

"Well, it's hard to imagine Lou Gehrig writing books
after he retires from baseball. *Leaves of Grass* by Lou
Gehrig. *Much Ado About Nothing* by Lou Gehrig."

Rivers laughed at the same time that he looked ner-
vously at the privy marked Men. "Yeh, or *The Comedy of*

37

Errors."

"Ha."

"So you want to write too."

Fred regretted he'd let it slip out. "Yeh."

"Plays?"

"No. I was a member of the Thespian Club in college but plays weren't for me."

"Why not?"

"I'm never convinced it's real up there on the stage. I can't get taken in. Like I do in movies. Or in a good novel."

Rivers hopped around on one leg while holding himself back. "Novels then?"

"I started one once but when I let a girl in college read it, she hooted at the way I described women."

"Why?"

"They weren't real, she said. Too many petticoats."

"Don't tell me you're still a virgin."

Fred blushed. "Mostly it's that I had no sisters."

"About time for you then to dunk your doughnut."

"There's more to it than that."

"Well sure. But . . ."

Fred shivered. He had to go bad too. "Mostly I've written poems."

"There's no money in that."

"I know."

Rivers kept looking at the men's privy. "Tell you. Go to New York. You'll meet other writers there. The excitement of meeting other creative minds will be good for you. And meet women. Women of talent you can go to bed with."

Fred had a little smile. "Your wife Joan hasn't got a sister, has she?"

Rivers gave him a strangled look.

Just then the father and the three boys emerged from

38

the men's privy.

"Good!" Rivers exclaimed, and with a skip and a jump headed for it. "C'mon."

"No. You go ahead." Fred was shy about going to a bathroom with strangers.

The father and his three boys headed for the outdoor pump. The father began working the pump handle while his boys took turns drinking from a tin cup.

Rivers soon emerged from the men's privy. "Okay. She's all yours now."

Fred took his turn next. He closed the door after him. It was dusky inside, light coming from the cracks in the wall and the quarter-moon cut in the door. Shyly he held his hand over his private parts as though someone might be present.

The south wind gave the door a hard shove. With his free hand Fred shoved it closed again.

The truck driver blew his horn, twice, sharp. "Time to get rolling," he called out.

"Wow. I better hurry," Fred murmured to himself. "I guess I waited too long."

Fred thought it a kind of cosmic irony that while one part of a man could be dreaming of writing poems another part of him could be busy eliminating waste.

There were footsteps outside and then a rap on the privy door. "You still in there?" It was the truck driver.

"Yep."

"Better come now. I've got to get back to the ranch before dark."

"Okay. I'll be right out."

Fred buttoned up. Then outside again, as he passed the pump, he quick had himself a cup of water.

When he got into the truck he was surprised to discover that a newcomer, a young hobo, had taken over his spot beside the Rivers couple. Fred considered the fellow a moment, then said, "I'm sorry, but you're standing in my place." He was about to point to his suitcase standing against the rack, when he discovered it had been set in the middle of the truck.

The hobo sneered at him. "Too bad, bud."

Fred made a move as though to push in anyway.

The young hobo instantly flashed fierce gray teeth at him, at the same time that his right fist, clenched white, popped into view, not an inch away from Fred's nose. "Back off, bud."

Fred retreated a step. "Some people's kids sure got manners."

"Make something of it. Go ahead."

Rivers and Joan, and all the others aboard the truck, watched to see what Fred would do about it.

Well, Gramma would say he should be the bigger man. Fred smiled a little to himself. Of course if it came to a fight he could easily beat the tar out of the fellow. The bum could never be a match for one who knew how to box and who'd once lifted a thousand pounds of shelled corn off the ground. Fred decided to let it go for the moment.

The trucker stepped on the starter. The engine fired instantly and in a moment, with a lurch and a grinding of gears, they were off.

Fred straddled himself over his suitcase, legs wide apart to keep his balance.

Joan pointed back down the highway. "Is that the corn palace you talked about?"

Fred glanced around. A round mosque-like tower showed over the trees. It had a sun-darkened yellow color. "That's it, I guess."

Rivers said, "Strange to be seeing such a tower in this kind of country. Alien, really."

Fred nodded. "Not native, you mean.

40

Autochthonous, as my favorite prof would say."

The young hobo kept giving Fred the eye. He had the hard look of a much older man. The livid light in his grey eyes went on and off as if a kaleidoscope were slowly spinning inside his skull. His gaunt hollow cheeks had the look of weathered bacon. His lips resembled the just healed edges of a light knife cut. He had a loose Adam's apple. As the truck clattered down the ribbed gravel road his head bobbed like a turkey's. There was a sandblasted look about his overalls and shirt. In contrast he had on good workshoes, well-oiled, with thick soles, and the laces were still without knots.

They passed a farm where there'd once been a considerable mudhole around a water tank. South winds had so dried out the mud that cracks a half-foot wide zigzagged all through it. The skeletons of two cows lay bleaching near the tank. They'd been picked white by vultures.

"You see that?" Joan cried, horrified.

"Yeh," Rivers said.

"It's like looking into Dante's *Inferno.*"

"People are fools to live out here."

Fred said nothing. It was sobering to see those glistening white bones.

"Truly, a land of savages."

The hard-eyed hobo let go with a loud snort.

At Mt. Vernon they were suddenly back on smooth paving again. The terrible jolting gave way to a ride as smooth as a dream. Everybody smiled in relief. Joan adjusted her underclothes through her yellow dress. The woman sitting with her back to the red cab did the same.

The young hobo leaned over the side of the rack a while, looking down at the passing tar road. Then, as if he'd come to some kind of conclusion, he turned to

Fred. "Hell, come on, I'll move over a little. You can stand here too."

Fred wasn't too sure he wanted to accept the offer. Anyone subject to such abrupt shifts in mood wasn't the best kind of riding partner, especially close up.

The young hobo moved over a good full step. "Come on."

"Oh, all right." Fred picked up his suitcase and advanced to the side of the rack. What a relief to be able to hold on to something.

Fred could feel both Rivers and Joan quietly studying the hardmouth fellow. They too had their private thoughts.

The hobo looked down at Fred's red sweater. "You one of them college bums?"

"Yes. Sorry."

"Well, my cousin went to college too and he managed to turn out all right."

"Where you from?"

"Oklahoma." The fellow more threw his words over his shoulder than spoke directly at Fred. "That's where they really had a black blizzard."

"So I heard."

"Man! Down there we had human skeletons laying around water tanks. Like a necklace of white pearls. Yeh, it was a roughty all right."

Fred saw the young fellow had his good side too.

"My mother and father died from it. Christ."

"Sorry to hear that."

"Nothing one could do about it though. It's time to get out when even the wild animals leave a country."

They rolled through Plankinton.

Fred began to feel very hungry. He pulled out the rest of the candy bar and opened the folded over end of it. Before taking a bite, he offered the young man a piece of it.

43

The hardmouth stared at the bit-off end; then, wetting his lips, took the candy bar, opened the wrapper at the other end, broke off a bite, almost a third of it, and handed it back. "Thanks."

Fred finished the rest of the bar.

Cracks in the earth began to show up everywhere, not just in the mudholes. Sometimes the fissures were deep, and angled in every possible direction across the passing fields. The earth had the odd look of a huge apple that had dried too fast.

Near White Lake, on the edge of town, they passed what had once been a huge pond. The old pond bed was so scorched that its cracked cakes of dried mud were frosted over with a sugarlike icing. Several of the cracks had fissured out across the road. In two places the tar paving had separated a good four inches. The trucker had to slow down for them. The several cracks in the earth jolted the riders.

The bronze haze in the west continued to thin out as they approached it. What had once looked like a distant dust storm now appeared to be a holy ambience of a rawgold texture. Dreamlike. Otherworldly.

The black water tower of Kimball came into view just as the tar road changed back to roughboard gravel. The ribbed road worked on bonejoints once more.

"Where you headed?" the hardmouth fellow asked.

"West. Nowhere in particular. Just see the sights."

"That's me. I've already been through here a couple of times looking for work. I just ramble back and forth liked a tumbleweed."

"Say, my name is Fred."

"Mine's Beeford."

"That a first name?"

"Hell, no. I don't give out my first name. My ma gave me one but I never liked it. So I dropped it." Beeford stared at the label on Fred's sweater and tried to read the lettering. "Frederick Feek . . . what the hell kind of name is that?"

There it was again. Always the damned problem of the American tongue not being able to pronounce Feikema. "I suppose you could say it's Dutch. Though it's really Frisian."

"Christ, and here I always thought Beeford was a funny last name. But yours. Course Fred is all right. But Feek-e-ma?"

Fred gave Beeford a sheepish grin. It was best to laugh such things off. He couldn't blame people. Though he himself never felt alien. He felt American. In the country school he'd gone to the first five grades there'd never been any question that he belonged to the local earth north of Doon. "It's Fy′-ke-ma."

"Hm. Well, that way it don't sound too bad."

The road veered toward Pukwana, place where there'd once been a good smoke with a peacepipe. They entered the goldbrown ambience. Fine bits of brown dust floated in the air, just barely perceptible. It had an odor like stale old chocolate cake and a taste like rusting cast-iron.

Fred asked, "How do you pay your way?"

"Catch jobs where I can. Steal a chicken when I have to. And so long's it's summer I sleep outdoors. Never rains, you know."

Fred wasn't exactly flush with money himself, what with only eight dollars plus on him, seven of them in his shoe, but the thought of not knowing where one's next meal was going to come from, that was going pretty far.

The horizon began to change again. There was a rumpled look about it. And then, shortly, the edge of the earth ahead appeared to drop out of sight, away and down into a vast valley. In a moment, as the truck turned north a short distance, a broad running belt of

45

water shimmered into view.

"The Missouri River," Fred whispered.

"Really?" Joan cried.

"My God," Rivers said, "that's wider than the Hudson."

Beeford snorted.

The lowering sun made the river look like a vast sheet of burning silver. It was hard on the eye even as the eye kept circling back toward it.

"I never dreamed it'd be that big," Fred whispered.

The humpshouldered bluffs on both sides of the river were of a kind with the great stream. The bluffs were covered with tan grass and resembled two long windrows of huge sleeping mountain lions.

The truck turned left and they began to roll downhill, the engine murmuring, the tires whistling on smooth cement paving. The first homes of Chamberlain drifted by. Then came the edge of the downtown section and the rising approach to the silver suspension bridge.

As they rumbled across the river, Fred stared down at the vast sheet of moving water. It was tan in color, with small drifting whirlpools, bobbing logs, occasional half-soaked tumbleweeds, upboilings of ochreous sands. There was even a hugh live cottonwood bobbing along with its green leather leaves still cliddering in the breeze. The Missouri was the gathered up sum total of all flowing streams above. The Cheyenne. The Grand. The Yellowstone.

With a bump they left the long bridge. The truck picked up speed to climb the long road ahead as it snaked up through the folded bluffs. While they climbed everybody looked back. The vast river changed colors, subtly, tan turning to gray then to lightblue then to darkblue. Irregularly coursing ripples broke the flowing mirror.

Fred had the feeling that he'd passed through the lower reaches of a tremendous church, with far walls of browngold, with lofty ceilings of light floating gold, all of it suffused by the tawny music of a primitive stone organ.

They reached the top of the bluff line. A cinnamon sun lay almost level with their eyes. Darkbrown shadows reached across all the falling draws.

Rivers asked, "Where did he say he was going to turn off?"

"Kennebec," Fred said.

"Let's see that map of yours."

Fred got the map out and in the falling umber light they studied it together. "Let's see. Twenty-two miles to Reliance. Then fifteen miles to Kennebec. Thirty-seven more miles."

Rivers studied the sun. "It'll be about dusk then. Wonder if there's some kind of hotel there. Joan and I have just about had enough for today."

Fred studied the map some more. Despite the jiggling truck he made out that the name Kennebec was printed in darker letters than the names of the other towns around. "Looks to me like it's the county seat of Lyman County."

"Good. There's bound to be a hotel of some kind then. County commissioners'll certainly make sure of that."

Beeford broke in. "Not to forget the cowboys."

"Oh? Is this cowboy land?" Joan asked. She got excited all over again.

Beeford waved his hand at the long flowing land. "Take a look for yourself. Don't see many farmsteads around here. It's pretty much all ranchland."

Joan placed a slender hand on Rivers' arm. "Maybe we can have dinner with a cowboy this evening, dear."

47

Rivers nodded. "That would be lovely."

Beeford snorted. "Dinner? Only city hicks call it that in the evening."

There were very few dust drifts. The roadside ditches were clearly defined. The old unplowed prairie sod held the soil in place.

In Reliance the buildings had a curious architecture. Most homes appeared to be made of several shacks stuck together. The whole town had a ramshackle look. Apparently the first pioneers had tried farming in the area and then, after repeated crop failures, had quit and moved their shacks to town.

The bumpy gravel road became smooth tar paving with several miles yet to go to Kennebec.

"That's better," Fred said, sighing. His belly hurt and he was tired of all the beating his bones had taken.

Rivers allowed himself a smile. "County commissioners probably also saw to that. Making sure the county seat would have good roads leading to it."

The black cylinder water tower of Kennebec hung in the sky directly above a round red sun.

The trucker slowed at the Kennebec corner, turned right, and headed up the main street. He pulled up in front of some gas tanks outside a garage. The motor fell to a mumble, backfired and coughed, and fell silent.

The trucker swung out on the runningboard. "Well, folks, this is as far as I go on 16. I live north of here."

Everybody got down, the five harvest hands, the family of five, Rivers and his wife Joan, and last Fred and Beeford. The family of five and the five grain hands headed for a bean palace called Min's Cafe across the street.

Rivers looked at Fred. "Care to join us for dinner at the hotel?"

"I think I'll just have me a bite to eat in that cafe

across there."

"Aren't you going to stay over in the hotel?"

"No, I think I'm going to try for some more rides yet before dark."

"Oh." Joan more than Rivers appeared to be disappointed. "Well, suit yourself."

"Sorry."

"Remember now. Go to New York the first chance you get. You're ready for it."

"Okay."

Rivers and Joan trudged up the street.

Beeford tugged at Fred's elbow. "You really gonna eat in that cafe?"

"Yeh. Just a hamburger."

"You got the velvet?"

"I got me a roll as big as a wagon hub."

"So long." Beeford turned and headed back for Highway 16.

Fred watched him go a few steps. The fellow didn't even have a bindle he was so hard up. Sometime during the evening some chicken coup down the road would be minus a rooster. "Hey, wait up."

Beeford kept striding away.

"Wait up. I'll buy you a hamburger."

"I ain't takin' charity." Beeford snapped the words over his shoulder. "The hell with that."

"C'mon."

"No." Beeford hurried on, looking east to see if there might not be a car or truck coming.

Fred finally shrugged, then picked up his suitcase and headed across the street.

Min's Cafe wasn't much of a place. There was a smell about it as if it had once been a produce house, of eggs and sour cream.

The five grain hands sat lined up at the counter while

49

the family sat around a table in back. They were the only customers. A fat dumpling of a woman, the Min of the place, wasn't really happy at all the sudden business. There was a pinched grimace at the corners of her lips.

Fred mounted the end chair at the counter.

"Something for you?" Min asked.

"I'll have a hamburger and a malted."

Fred tried not to look at Min's bulging fat. He thought it funny that so fat a woman should live in so lean a country. Even her big greyblue eyes rolled in fat.

The hamburger turned out be a surprise. The paddy of meat was a half-inch thick and a good four inches across. The bun was also thick, with a good chunk of homemade butter smeared on both halves. It came with a large slice of dill pickle. And the malted was so rich it stood up almost like freshly made ice cream. Fred relished it all.

"Anything else?"

"Yes. How about a nice glass of water?"

"That'll be another dime."

"What!"

The other ten customers looked up. They weren't so much surprised by Fred's exclamation as they were by the fact that a glass of water in Kennebec cost a dime.

"You're charging for water?" Fred went on.

"Got to. It costs us to have it hauled in from the Missouri River."

"My God."

"Sorry. But that's the way it is." Min licked her thick lips. "We're all but dusted out of here, you know."

"I'll go without the water then." Fred stood up. He checked the loose change in his pocket and saw he didn't have quite enough. He dug out his billfold and handed her the single dollar bill in it.

Min took the bill and looked at it a moment.

50

"It ain't counterfeit," Fred said, lips twisting a little.

"I ain't worried about that. It's that I maybe don't have the change." She rang up the amount, 25¢, on the cash register. The drawer banged open with an empty sound. She fingered through the several little compartments, finally came up with a handful of nickels and pennies. She counted them out. The broad calloused pad of her forefinger was larger than the pennies she pushed toward Fred. " . . . eighty, eighty-five, ninety, ninety-five, one dollar."

Fred stared at the pile of copper and nickel-silver.

One of the nearby hands allowed himself an interested smile. "Looks like you're about ready to open a bank with all that cash on hand."

"Yeh. I'm going to have to get me a cart to haul all that around with me," Fred said.

"That's the way it is," Min said flatly.

Fred cupped up the copper and nickel coins and dropped them into his trouser pocket. The money lay on his thigh like a warm brick. Then he picked up his suitcase and stepped outside.

The sun was down. The whole west horizon was streaked with a series of rising cathedrals of color, most of them a brilliant transparent citron. Main street had the look of the promised golden streets of heaven.

Fred walked toward the highway. He saw that Beeford still hadn't caught a ride.

Beeford greeted him with a little curl of lips. He first looked at Fred's belly, then his eyes.

Fred set down his suitcase on the shoulder of the tar road beside Beeford. "No cars I see."

"Not even a cowboy on a horse."

"Getting pretty late in the day, actually."

"There still might be an empty cattle truck coming back from Iowa."

51

Fred watched the citron cathedrals in the west change to a whole shining range of fantasy mountains leaning off to the north. Very high winds were at work shaping different atmospheres of fine dust.

Beeford had a further sneer. "Ain't you gonna sleep with that New York pair in the hotel tonight?"

"Where are you going to sleep tonight?"

"Where else but on the ground. That's been my only bed the past year."

"That should be good enough for me then too."

Beeford liked what he heard. "Listen, bo. I got a plan. Care to join me?"

Fred was afraid of what was coming next. "Yeh?"

"The last time I was through here I found out that from Chamberlain on they close down the passenger trains on one side. All the depots are on the same side of the tracks from here to the Hills. We can ride all the way sitting on those steps on the blind side. Train comes through here around four in the morning."

Fred considered the idea. What with the dust already flying plus the black soot from the engine, it was going to make for a pretty gritty ride. "You sure?"

"I did it before." Beeford stood with one hand in pocket scratching his thigh through cloth. "Course we got to be careful how we hop aboard. We don't want the local station master to see us standing alongside the tracks waiting for the train or he'll call the railroad dick. When it gets pitch dark, we'll walk over and go tucky-bed a couple blocks from the tracks. When the train stops we'll sneak up in the dark and hop on."

Fred glanced down at his neatly pressed pants. "This'll get pretty grimy."

"Well, it's your butt."

The fantasy mountain range faded away. In a few minutes darkness out of the east rushed west to shut down the whole world.

Lights came on in the town behind them. Most were the weak lights of kerosene lamps. The only electric lights on were those in the windows downtown.

"Well," Beeford said, shoving both hands into his pockets and making bulges of them, "about time we hunted us up our featherbeds."

"Yeh, I suppose there's no use waiting here."

Beeford led the way. He took a circuitous route around the west side of town, well out of range of the lamps of the houses. Presently they hit the railroad tracks. The tracks lay flat on the prairie without an embankment.

Fred almost fell down carrying his suitcase. "Cripes, what a guy won't do to save a buck."

Beeford pushed his toes carefully across the windblasted sod. "I was hoping that somewhere along here we'd find a little depression we could hide in. But no such luck. Well, we'll just walk out a little farther to make sure the big eye don't pick us out."

"Big eye?"

"Yeh, you know. The headlight on the steam engine."

Fred followed blindly after. He'd once heard there were rattlers on the west side of the Missouri. He hoped that the occasional soft lumps he felt with the toes of his oxfords were horseballs, not sleeping rattlesnakes.

"This is far enough," Beeford said. His face, a gray oval in the brown darkness, was barely visible. He made a little scurrying circle like a dog looking for the right place to light in, then knelt down and with a groan stretched himself out on the ground. "Ah, in bed at last. After a hard day's work."

Fred considered getting out his beautiful maroon blanket and spreading that out on the bare earth, but

53

then remembered that the week before he'd had that cleaned.

"Can't you find your spot?"

Fred stooped and felt around with his fingers. "I'm okay." A couple of steps on the other side of Beeford his fingertips found a small plot of dried grass. The grassy plot didn't feel too dusty. It would have to do. He lay down. Using his suitcase as a pillow, he stretched out. "Ah, bed at last."

"Sweet dreams."

"Yeh."

There was just enough dust riding to blot out the Milky Way.

"I could do with a woman," Beeford said, more to himself than to Fred.

Fred said nothing. He wondered what Rivers and Joan were doing. Rivers was probably right at that moment making love to voluptuous Joan. But Fred didn't envy Rivers. He'd much rather spend a platonic evening with That Special Face back in Grand Rapids. He and Special Face would be soft as violets touching each other. Reciting poems to each other. Making up their own poems for each other.

"When's the last time you had it?" Beeford asked in the dark.

Fred had never done it. But he could hardly admit it to hardnose Beeford. Beeford wouldn't believe him. Unless Beeford meant masturbation. Or even worse, unless Beeford was a queer. The last thought made Fred stiffen. He'd run into one such fellow while hitchhiking from Calvin College to Chicago. Fred had been so shocked at the time that for a while he'd had trouble getting his breath and his heart had skipped occasional beats.

"It's been a month of Sundays for me." A rustling

54

noise came from Beeford as though he were playing pocket pool. "But God, was that last one a good one. Man man. The way I put the blocks to her . . . och!" Beeford bounced up and down several times in memory. "I can hardly stand to think about it."

Fred stared up at the few stars. He couldn't imagine what kind of memory Beeford was having. It certainly had to be a whole lot more satisfying than that time he himself and the hired girl had tried fumblingly to make connection, first on the horsechair sofa and later that same night on the kitchen floor. It was a memory he didn't particularly care to dwell on. Too furtive. Too guilt-ridden. Too sad all around.

"You got a sweetie back home?" Beeford asked.

Fred said nothing.

Beeford sighed. Sighed twice. "Well, I had one once. I learned with her. And she learned with me. The first time we did it, why, it was like our brains fell out. Man."

"Was she a neighbor girl?"

"Yeh. How'd you know?"

"Just wondering."

"Yeh. She lived across the road from us. We always walked a mile and a half to school together. It's a long ways to go to school in Oklahoma. We were into everything together. You see, we were only kids and so had nobody else to play with."

"What happened? Where's she now?"

There was a sound in the dark of Beeford stretching his arms.

"Sorry. Didn't mean to pry."

"It's okay, bo." Beeford made a noise as though he were licking dry lips. "Haven't thought about Ellen in quite a while. Had so many women since she's almost washed out of my mind." Beeford coughed, once, softly.

"We was about to get married when the big dust storms came. She commenced to cough about then. She coughed and coughed. Like to coughed her gizzard out. Come winter she died of pneumonia. About then my folks lost their farm to a mortgage company. No crops, no money. My folks went to town and lived on relief, and me, I went on the bum. The next time I came by, my paw and maw had died. I think they just up and quit. From a broken heart, you might say."

"Cripes," Fred said. Fred didn't know which was worse, having a dead lost sweetie or a live lost sweetie. After some further thought Fred decided maybe the bum had it the worst. The bum had lost a sweetie with whom he'd made love, while he'd only lost a sweetie with whom he'd exchanged a dry good-bye kiss.

"Yeh, it was roughty."

Fred asked, "There wasn't a baby on the way, was there?"

"Not that I know of."

"That last one you had, where did you run into her?"

"She was a small town teacher. She told me she was just out tooling around in her Chevy. About thirty. Just hadn't quite run into the right man yet. She pulled up where I was standing, looked at me fer about a minute sizin' me up, and then asked where I was going. Well, I knew right away what was troubling her. So I told her it was just to the next town. So she nodded for me to get in." Beeford sucked in his lips.

"Then what?"

"Well, we tooled on down the road. Pretty soon she said, 'I wonder, would you mind if we'd first go have a look to see if the plums are ripe along the river?' And I said, 'Not at all.' She said, 'You like plums, don't you?' And I said, 'I sure do.' So we stopped by the river. Then as we got out of the car and started for the plum trees,

56

we bumped into each other, and then, for a fact, in about two minutes it was over."

"God."

"Yeh. It was sweet. We did it twice. The second time was the best. Because it lasted an hour."

"Then what?"

"Nothing. She took me to the next town and then she went back home."

"You mean, she did it like an animal might? No regrets?"

"Yep. It's best to do it with a stranger, you know. That way no one will ever find out about it. I didn't ask her name and she didn't mine. Besides, it's best when you do it like an animal."

Fred lay picturing the scene.

"Well," Beeford said, "for now I guess all I can do is cross my legs and pinch off the brain."

"If you could get a job, would you settle down?"

"Too late. I've been ruined for work."

"Don't you want to get ahead?"

"Ahead to what?"

"Well, you know, make a success of yourself?"

"Listen, bo, I'm pretty good at what I'm doing right now."

"But that's not what a man would call work."

Beeford sighed. "Bo, it's too late for me. I've gotten used to being free as the wind."

"Oh."

"I guess you think I'm pretty low."

"I didn't say that."

"Yeh, I can just feel myself getting worse every day. And one of these days I'll be lower than whaleshit on the bottom of the ocean."

Fred almost laughed. He thought that remark quite a conceit.

"Well, time to turn in. Night."

"Good-night."

The wind died down completely. Fred could feel an occasional large particle of dust settle on his face. He licked his lips now and then.

The patch of grass felt pretty good. Gradually Fred slipped off into sleep.

He awakened feeling cold. He listened in the night. Beeford was breathing slowly and heavily a little ways off. An involuntary shiver coursed up Fred's body. At last, with a sigh, hating to stir, Fred sat up, and opening his suitcase, got out his maroon blanket. Closing the suitcase again, and lying down, he spread the blanket carefully over himself.

That was better. The blanket instantly lay warm over him.

He dreamed up at the dark night for a while. He felt something in the corner of his right eye. With a finger he pried it out. Dust dingle. He gave it a pinch. It was gritty with the finest of sands. Sand so fine it could float on air.

Presently he heard a sound under him. He listened closely. Why! the whole earth under him was humming a single organ note. Continuous and alto. He'd never heard that before. But it was there all right. He wasn't going nuts. Everything had quieted down, the wind, animals moving, cars moving, people moving, everything, and with his ear against the earth he was really hearing it.

It thrilled him. He wished Special Face or John were there so he could share the marvelous discovery with them.

It made him wonder after a while if he himself didn't have a sound. Personal and his own. He lay even quieter, stiller, almost stiffening, straining to hear the better. But all he could hear was that low powerful pervasive alto sound of a turning brown earth.

Too bad he'd never taken music. It would be wonderful to get that sound into a piece of music. Build a symphony out of it. He'd call it The Found Chord.

He became aware that the wind had changed. He pushed out the tip of tongue. It was coming out of the northwest. He snuggled under his maroon blanket. And doing so, he lost the alto sound of the earth. And slept.

IV

A kick on his foot awoke him. Then the sound of a steam engine hooting, whistling eerily, came from the east beyond his toes. Opening his eyes, Fred saw that a very light streak of gray had begun to spread out across the eastern sky.

He next became aware of a pushing cold draft against his right hip. It was curious that it should be on that side when the wind was on the other side.

He lifted his head to have a look. It couldn't be wind getting under his blanket. But it was too dark to make out. He slid his hand over to find out what it could be. And felt something that scared the wits out of him. Coiled. Roughish. Like a scaled fishskin. Hey, a rattler. The shock stilled him. Scared to move, he eased his head down.

"Get up, bo. Time to catch our free ride to the Hills, you know." It was Beeford standing above him ready to kick his foot again.

Fred managed to throw a glance in the direction of the coiled up snake.

"I know it's hard to get up in the morning," Beeford said. "But just think how lucky we are. We don't have to work today. Just ride. In style too, on a train."

Again Fred threw a look in the direction of the snake, crossing his brows. Fred even pursed the corner of his lips toward the snake.

Beeford caught the frightened look on Fred's face. He stooped a little to look.

Fred waited. Beeford would think of something. Fred felt prickles going all up and down his right side. There was a feeling the prickles were coming in pairs, like snakebites.

Beeford straightened up. He looked off to one side

61

with a funny sneering kind of smile.

Fred shot another meaningful look at his right side. He thought: "For godsakes do something. Get a stick or something and flip it away from me."

The sneer on Beeford's thin lips deepened.

Fred thought he could feel the rattler stirring against him. In a minute it'd strike him and he'd be a dead duck.

The train whistled again, very loud. As its headlight pierced down the track it began to light up the area around Fred and Beeford a little.

The whistle made up Beeford's mind. He gave Fred a disgusted look, and began to head for the tracks.

Fred couldn't believe it. Beeford was deserting him.

The train stopped by the depot a minute. Then, two toots, it began to move again, the drivers on the great wheels slowly stroking faster and faster. There was a final toot at a crossing, and then the sound of the rattling passenger cars gradually faded off into the night.

Fred lay absolutely stiff. The chill of the rattler began to spread all through him. It even pushed up into his head.

At the same time, in a far corner of his brain, a part of him was having a quiet Chaucer smile at what was happening. The Chaucer in him knew his life was getting out of hand, that he was having trouble keeping up with what was going on, that all was turning to ashes, that he was falling through a grate . . . and yet that part could smile.

Then Fred thought: "Wait. Calm. Easy does it. If I can lie here long enough without moving, pretty soon the sun'll come up and it'll warm the snake and then the snake'll crawl off somewhere. Sure. And then I can go back to thumbing rides."

Fred prepared himself to lie still for a long while.

He thought of tiny Special Face. But a lot of good that did. Even if she'd been there with him in person she wouldn't have been of much help. What could she have done?

He wondered if he shouldn't just pray. Though it was silly to think God would stop whatever He was doing at that moment and reach down with His scepter and flick the snake away. Were Christ still on earth that would be another matter. But not God the Almighty Himself.

He tried to imagine his brothers sleeping in sweet innocence in their two beds back home — if they could only see their oldest brother lying on the open prairie in South Dakota and about to die.

The sky lightened over Fred. Black became gray became pink. The town behind him began to awaken too. Somewhere on one of the streets someone started up a truck. The truck motor spit and missed and popped. It took a while for the motor to level out. It finally backfired a few times, roared up, and then took hold. Gears were shifted twice. Slowly the motor began to whine. Then came the sound of wheels bumping. Then came the smooth purr of rubber on tar. The sound of it went west. There probably went his one good ride for the day.

The sky lightened even more. The sun popped over the horizon and pink was displaced by piercing yellow shafts of light. The sun shone on him and shortly his chin began to feel warm. He could feel the sun brush over his brow, his hair.

He kept breathing even and low.

It was when the sun began to shine on his throat, warm and loving, that he at last felt movement in the rattlesnake. It was as though someone were stirring a cold pudding tight against him. His ears cracked. He could hear harsh dry skins sliding past each other. The

63

snake began to move. Slowly the piled up cold coils of the snake fell away. Faintly came the sound of dust being touched, brushed over lightly. There was a wisp of sound as though the rattles were being ruffled.

He wasn't sure just when the snake had finally pulled away from him. He didn't dare move his head the slightest bit until he was absolutely sure the snake had crawled off far enough for him to make his move. He waited until the sensation of being cold on his right hip had disappeared; and then waited still a while longer.

He made his move all in one rising bound. He sprang free of the grassy plot, blanket falling in a heap at his feet. His heart beat so hard it jarred his vision for a few moments. He began to puff like a runner after a hard run.

He kicked a large stone loose from the dry hard soil, picked it up, and went looking for the rattler. He looked under a still-rooted tumbleweed, a tuft of joint grass, a cluster of stones. No rattler. It had mysteriously vanished. He didn't like to hurt creatures, hated to kill, but that rattler was another matter.

He went back and picked up his maroon blanket. He gave it a good shaking, picking off a few blades of dry grass, and then refolded it and put it neatly in his suitcase again. As he did so he noted that the grass he'd slept on was a little patch of buffalo grass. It was short and curly, very much like the tawny hair of an old buffalo robe.

He next brushed off his clothes. To make sure the back of his maroon sweater was clean, he slipped it off and gave it a good shaking too. He picked off several bits of grass. He slipped it back on again with an easy shrugging motion. He brushed back his hair. Satisfied that he looked as neat as ever, he picked up his suitcase and headed for town.

64

Min's Cafe was open. A single customer sat at the counter. Heavy dumpling Min with her thick greyblue eyes was waving a spatula over the stove in back.

Fred set his suitcase down and mounted the stool next to the single customer. The single customer gave him a brief impersonal glance; went back to sipping his coffee.

Min trundled over. "What'll it be?"

Fred still felt chilled from the touch of the rattler. "Coffee. And how much are your doughnuts?"

"Two for a nickel."

"I'll have that."

Min poured him some steaming coffee. She got two doughnuts out from under a glass cover and set them on a plate before him. "Will that be it?"

Fred nodded.

"Ten cents then."

"That include seconds on coffee?"

"What else?"

Fred fell silent. He thought it a bit odd that she'd charge ten cents for a glass of water and only a nickel for two cups of coffee. He dug out a dime for her.

He was into his second doughnut and second cup of coffee when he noticed the other customer's clothes. The fellow was wearing a sort of uniform, gray neat shirt and gray neat trousers with a black belt and black work shoes. The fellow also had on a black leather cap. A clipboard thick with sheets of paper lay nearby on the counter. Fred could make out some words in what looked like a government report. "Geological formations of the West River Country." The fellow was a scientist of some kind then. Maybe even someone who worked for the federal government.

Fred finished the last of his coffee.

The other customer lit up a tailormade Lucky Strike, then held out the pack to Fred, giving it a little shake so that a single white cigarette slid out an inch. "Care for a smoke?"

Fred considered the lovely white tube of tobacco. What a temptation. "No, I better not."

The fellow glanced at Fred's sweater. "C stand for Cornell?"

"No. Calvin."

"Where's that?" The fellow put his cigarettes away.

Fred smiled a little. Just as with his name Feikema, he usually had to explain about Calvin College too. He told the fellow a little about Calvin and the denomination supporting it.

"I've heard about that sect." The fellow had a quiet square face with a set of level grey eyes. "What are you doing out here?"

"Seeing the country. On my way to Yellowstone."

"You're seeing it at its worst."

"I guess I am getting a good look at the Dust Bowl at that."

"My name's Overacker."

"I'm Fred Feikema. Glad to meet you."

Overacker didn't blink at Fred's name. He saw Fred glance at the clipboard. "I'm a geologist making a survey for the government. So you're headed west. Want a ride?"

"Sure do."

"Good. I'm going as far as Vivian. Then I'm headed south to check out the White River valley. Near Vera."

Overacker dinched out his cigarette and got up. Fred got up to go too. Min called after them, as they headed for the door, "Don't forget to come back."

Overacker drove a new black Chevie with a government insignia on the front door. The engine turned over on the first push of the starter button. In a moment they were headed west on 16.

Fred said, "Am I glad to leave that town."

"How so?"

Fred told about the rattler.

Overacker said, "Actually, you wouldn't have had to wait until it crawled away. It wasn't coiled to strike; it was coiled to sleep. And being cold it couldn't have struck you. No leverage. And even if it did make a little pecking motion, it could never have penetrated your skin."

"If I'd only known that. Well, live and learn."

They rolled west. The sun shone warm through the rear window of the car. It was calm out. The sky was a very light blue, as though at any moment something special might happen.

Overacker pointed. "See that curving row of what look like little toy mesas going over that rise?"

"Yeh."

"Those are footsteps."

"What?"

"A cow walked there after a rain some years ago. She pressed the mud down just hard enough so that when the wind came her footsteps were the last to erode."

Some of the little footstep mesas had been honed so thin by the wind they resembled black mushrooms.

"The area around here has had only a total of an inch of rain in the last two years."

"No wonder."

"Last November was the worst I ever saw it out here. People spoke of it as the Great Black Blizzard."

Fred nodded. "I remember reading about it. And the funny thing is, some of us in Grand Rapids thought the air there was bad."

"Very likely. Some of that Dakota dust even landed in the Atlantic."

The black tower of Presho lifted out of the flat

horizon ahead.

In several of the shallow valleys people had tried farming. The houses all looked deserted, windows broken in, doors flapping open. In one barn a gaunt black horse stood in the doorway. The horse had a look as though it had just got out of bed and was wondering out at the world trying to decide if it was worth being alive.

Overacker shook his head at the farmsteads. "Should never've been plowed. Should've remained what it once was, cattle country."

"You mean, big spreads."

"Right. Presho up ahead there, you know, was once the bedding down place for big round-ups. It was also a great haying country."

"Where'd they get the water?"

"Medicine Creek. That draw down there is always wet. Even today, for some reason."

They rolled past the south edge of Presho. It too had a dust-blasted look.

The paving continued and the black Chevie tooled along as smooth as a slowly swinging hammock. The sharp sun cast dark shadows behind every fence post.

"What I miss is the birds," Fred said.

"There's still some around. Down in the draw there along the creek. Meadowlarks. Song sparrows."

"And vultures."

"Yes, those too."

They rode in silence for a good ways, each with his own thoughts, looking at the sere landscape lifting up and then letting down in long smooth slopes.

Fred wondered if Overacker was married, and if he was, what sort of husband he made. Fred had trouble imagining Overacker making love to a woman.

Again That Special Face came to mind. There was

something wonderful about sorrowing over a lost love. Sometimes it was fun to feel sad. Sadness was like having found a new faith. The sad feeling probably wouldn't save one. But someone, another womanly being, was sure to come along to comfort one.

Vivian appeared on the next rise. It rose out of the sweep of land as if it were a magic city hanging in the western sky. It lay spread out on a climbing hill, on the highest part of which stood a tall brick high school. Behind the schoolhouse on a still higher hill stood a white water tower.

Overacker said, "There's a State Experiment Farm on the other side of town." Overacker shook his head to himself. "But I fear it's a case of throwing away the taxpayer's money. It'll soon be closed down."

A tumbleweed lay in the middle of the road. There wasn't enough wind out to move it. Overacker drove around it.

Overacker stopped at the corner of the main street. "I turn south here."

Fred got out his suitcase from the backseat and stepped down. "Thanks a lot for the lift."

"Don't mention it. And good luck."

"Yep."

V

Fred walked north through Vivian. He was surprised to see the town still had old-time boardwalks. Most homes were one story with roofed porches. A moaning sound, lonely and not of the wind, moved between the dwellings. The backyards were desolate. It hurt to look around the corners of the dust-scoured houses.

A young girl just barely nubile, blond hair done up in a long fat pigtail, pedaled past him on a girl's bike. An old gaunt woman came out on the porch with her broom and stared at him. When he was some two doors down she briskly began to sweep off her share of the boardwalk.

He took turns carrying his suitcase first in his right hand and then in his left hand. His right hip still felt cold where the rattler had lain against him. He hitched along a little as though he'd gone lame on that side.

He entered the little business district. Railroad tracks dissected it. He heard a gas engine running in a gun-metal grain elevator on the right.

The white depot on the left was deserted. Beyond it stood a single boxcar on a siding. The tracks were shiny. It meant an occasional train still came through town.

He decided to get himself a candy bar to eat for lunch later on. He entered a Standard Oil station. Used oil cans stood in exact rows on the floor against the far wall. The ceiling and the walls shone with a light-blue paint.

The attendant, a young blond fellow, sat in a swivel chair at a beat-up desk. He looked up, "I didn't hear you drive in."

Fred smiled, "I walked in."

"That explains it."

"Got any candy bars?"

"Over in the counter there." The young fellow got to

his feet and opened the glass top. "Help yourself."

Fred selected an O'Henry again. As he did so his eye fell on cigarette makings, a sack of Genuine Durham Smoking Tobacco, with an orange packet of Rizla+ cigarette papers attached. Sight of it instantly made him crave for a sweet silver smoke. He licked his lips. He was probably never going to get rid of that damnable habit. "How much is the Bull Durham?"

"Ten cents."

"I'll take one."

"Want another full packet of papers to go with it? They're eight cents a piece and two for fifteen."

"No, thanks." Fred had more than enough change left to pay for both items. He slid the candy bar into his pocket. When he tried to open the orange packet he discovered the thin delicate papers were stuck together along one edge. He had to blow gently to get them to separate. He finally managed to free one. He shook some powdery tobacco into the paper, caught one of the strings of the tobacco sack between his teeth and pulled the sack shut, dropped the sack into his pocket, and then expertly shook the tobacco level in the curved up paper and rolled it all up into a neat tube. He licked along the open edge, sealed it, twisted one end shut, then caught the other end between his lips. The fragile paper instantly stuck to his wet lips. "Got a match?"

The attendant tossed him a small box of little wood matches.

Fred lit up, took a tremendous drag, blew out a perfect ring of smoke. "Ah. That's better." Even the imprinting of where the rattler had touched him began to wear off. "Don't you smoke?"

"Nope. I even feel a little ashamed selling the stuff."

"Well, every now and then I try to quit." Fred watched the gray ash creep up the tube of tobacco.

72

"Say, you won't mind if I try to catch a ride in your filling station here, will you?"

The young attendant sobered over. "Dad won't like it."

"Okay. I'll stand a little ways up the street then. In front of the cafe there."

"Sorry."

Fred picked up his suitcase and sauntered out. He stepped over to the edge of the tar road and took up a hitchhiker's stance halfway between the station and the cafe.

Loose change almost gone, Fred took off his shoe and dug out another dollar bill and put it in his billfold.

The sun rose up over the elevator. There was still no wind out and it promised to be one of those rare days in Dakota when it would be utterly calm. The air in the town seemed to be filled with sounds: a car murmuring out of sight behind a house, the engine running in the grain elevator, a Fordson tractor popping far out on some ranch, a horse whinnying, a dozen children laughing with joy on the school grounds. Even the telegraph wires leading into the railroad depot hummed with wavering tunes.

Fred had just finished his second cigarette when an old car came wandering up main street from the south. The car moved as though the driver was not sure what to do next, stop for gas or drive on to the next town. Fred thought: "Aha. A ride maybe."

The old car jerked as the driver shifted down from high to second and rolled slowly across the tracks. It jerked again as the driver shifted down to low.

"Cripes," Fred muttered. "That's got to be a greenhorn."

The driver, a woman, was staring straight ahead with big wide brown eyes. Then she spotted the Standard Oil

73

station. Stiffly she rolled the wheel over and just barely managed to get the car straightened out as she pulled up in front of the gas pumps. She braked the car with a handbrake, hard, so that its tail came up with a loud squeak. The motor choked dead.

The woman driver sat very still. It took her a moment to collect her wits.

The old car she drove was a 1926 Essex, two-door, gray, with a shiny nickel radiator. It had an Illinois license plate. The back seat was full of suitcases.

"Good," Fred thought, "from Illinois she's bound to be driving through. I'll wait until she's gassed up and then I'll trot out the old winning smile and the handsome thumb."

The station attendant came around to the driver's side of the old Essex. "Fill'er up?"

The woman stared down at her dashboard. "Yes." She read something stuck to her windshield. "And oh, would you check the oil too, please?"

"Of course. I always do that."

She picked up her purse and stepped out. She brushed down her dress in back several times. She was about forty, of medium height, stocky. The skin over her hands and face had the white look of one who lived mostly indoors. She was well-dressed in a somewhat severe style, brown pleated skirt and tan blouse, tan stockings and brown shoes, a tight round black hat. The clothes set off her brown eyes, large, highly expressive, one moment timorous, the next moment snappish sharp. Her lips were set in a severe thin line.

The attendant unscrewed the cap from the Essex gas tank and inserted a long nickle nozzle and pressed a lever. Gas gushed into the tank.

"Do you, uh . . ." the woman began hesitantly, "uh, have a ladies room?"

74

"Yes. Behind in back there."

"Thank you." She took a few steps; stopped. "I don't suppose you have running water in it?"

"Are you joking? We sometimes don't even have water for your radiator."

"Oh."

"No, mam, it's just a plain outdoor backhouse."

She wrinkled her nose. "Thank you." Slowly she stepped around behind the station.

Fred began to wonder if he wanted a ride from such a creature. She looked like a dried-up old prune. Probably crabby as a broodhen.

The attendant next checked both the oil and water and found them all right. He carefully wiped the dusty windshield with a wet rag and then dried it with a shammy skin until the glass squeaked. Then he went inside to wait.

The woman returned. She moved somewhat furtive as though what she'd just gone through was something to be ashamed of. Just as she was about to step inside the station, she threw a look at Fred. The private furtive look vanished and her eyes sharpened to brown dots. She looked at him critically, from head to foot. Then she stepped inside.

Fred glanced up the street. No traffic. What a deserted world. Looking up he saw that all the fine riding particles of sand had disappeared. The great vault overhead had a high August blue. Licking his lips Fred for the first time in several days felt no gritty dust. With the sun out and very bright, and no wind, a happy time lay ahead.

Fred happened to glance back at the station, and through the glass made out that the woman and the attendant were talking about him. Every now and then they looked his way.

75

Fred narrowed his eyes. "Wonder what bank she thinks I robbed now."

There was some more talk between the two, and then the attendant stuck his head out of the door and called, "Want a ride?"

"Sure."

"Come on over a minute then. She wants to talk to you."

Fred picked up his suitcase and ambled into the station. He gave the woman a smile. "Don't tell me you're worried I won't fit in your car."

She looked him straight in the eye. Her brown eyes were cold and bright. She stood up stockily to him. "Yes, I could use a driver." She took a deep breath. "You see, I've just driven all the way from Chicago and I'm a little tired. And I thought that . . . well, if I saw a nice young college boy standing alongside the road looking for a ride, why, I'd give him a ride providing he'd drive for me."

Fred caught on. She knew she was a poor driver. "Where you going?"

She hesitated, looking off to one side. "Uh, I'm going as far as Murder."

"Murder!"

"I mean . . . Murdo."

"Oh."

"Are you a good driver?"

Fred thought of all the salesmen who'd picked him up in the past and who'd asked him to drive to some distant town ahead while they got in some sleep in the back seat. Fred had got so that he could drive any make of car. "Yes."

"Can you drive an Essex?"

"I've driven one. Though not so old a model."

"Aren't they all the same?"

"No. They change over the years. But I think I can handle your old crate."

The woman bristled. "I just bought it in Chicago. And they guaranteed it."

"I'm just kidding."

She stood up to him again. "But before I give you a ride I've got to know who you are. Can I know your name?"

Fred smiled. "I'm Frederick Feikema."

"Can you prove it?"

"For heavens sakes." He patted his various pockets. "I don't think so." Then he thought of the lettering on his maroon sweater. "Oh, I have this. I was given this sweater at Calvin College for playing basketball. My name was sewn on it. Here." He pulled his sweater around for her to read.

She leaned, peering. "Isn't that Dutch?"

"No. Frisian."

"Isn't that the same thing?"

"No. Calling a Frisian a Dutchman is like calling an Irishman an Englishman. Or a Basque a Spaniard."

"I see." Her eyes fixed on his. "Then you go to church?"

"Yes. I guess you can say that."

"You're not sure?"

"Yes, I'm sure."

"You see, young man, Mr. Feikema, I'm just not giving any old bum a ride in my car."

It was Fred's turn to bristle a little. "Look, lady, I didn't thumb you for a ride."

"Well now," she said, "let's not get our pride up."

"You called me over. I didn't you."

The young attendant's blue eyes darkened over.

The woman said, "Are you sure you don't have anything else on you to show who you are?"

Fred thought: "Well goldarn this woman. She's a lot like Aunt Kathryn, by golly." And thinking of Aunt Kathryn, Fred got an idea. He set down his suitcase, opened it, and dug out the letter he'd gotten from Aunt Kathryn two mornings before just as he was leaving home. He handed it over.

The woman eyed the envelope, eyed Fred, then with some delicacy extracted the single linen sheet. She read it slowly. When she finished she relaxed a little. She slipped the linen sheet back into the envelope and handed it back to him. "Your Aunt Kathryn sounds like a very nice lady. Very." She stood thinking to herself, looking down at the cement floor.

Fred noticed she had ink-stained fingertips. "Anything else you want to know?"

"No, not really. But I just wish I could be sure. I'm entrusting my life in your hands when I go down the road with you, you know."

"You mean, I might turn out to be a poor driver?"

"No, I mean, you might rape and murder me."

"Good God, woman." It was all Fred could do to keep from laughing right outloud.

She bristled once more. "You know very well the papers are full of it. The hiker kills the owner of the car sort of thing."

"Gosh, lady, I read the papers too and I don't remember reading that."

"Well I have, living in Chicago."

Fred felt a smile growing within him. She really was a case. "Well, Chicago, that's a crazy town. Gangster Al Capone and so on." Fred also recalled Red Huiner, a Calvin College student from Chicago. Red was the rascal who'd led a gang of sophomores during freshman hazing week and who'd painted his back red and then tied him to a post up in the attic of the Calvin Seminary.

78

The woman made up her mind. "I know what we can do. And then we can be on our way." She turned to the attendant. "You don't happen to have a piece of chalk handy, do you?"

The attendant was getting to be more and more upset by the fuss she was making. "Lady, what use have I got for a blackboard? This hain't a school."

"You're sure you don't have some kind of crayon I can make a mark with?" she persisted.

"Well, let me have a look around." He jerked open several drawers in an old beat-up desk. He was quite noisy about it. "Oh yeh. That reminds me." He fished through a used cigar box and came up with a slender piece of white chalk. "We sometimes use it to mark a nail hole in a tire casing."

"Good." She brightened. "Now. Would you" — she pointed to Fred — "would you line up against that wall there, and then you" — she gestured at the attendant — "trace his outline on that wall?"

"What the hell for?" the attendant cried.

She frowned darkly. "I don't like swearing."

"Well, what for then?"

"Should something happen to me, you'll know who did it from his outline." She glanced up at Fred's height. "There aren't very many tall men like him around."

"For crissake."

"Please."

Again Fred repressed laughter. "Wait." He winked at the attendant. "Lady, I'll let you make a map of me provided that you agree to something too."

She turned icy. "Provided what."

"You tell me your name. So the attendant here can hear it."

"But why?"

80

"I told you mine. Fair is fair."

"Well, but, a woman has more to lose than a man."

"But look at it from my point of view. I have to worry too that you might seduce me. And that would be a fate worse than death."

The attendant almost burst out laughing.

Fred went on. "In fact, I'll let this fellow draw a map of me, provided that you not only tell me your name but that he also draw a map of you on the same wall. That way in case my poor Christian father learns I've been seduced by a strange lady traveler he'll know who did it."

She stood very still. After a moment she appeared to swell up a little. She said evenly, "I'll never let any one draw a map . . . an outline of me." She bit on the inside of her lips. "But I do need a driver and so therefore I will give you my name. It's Miss Minerva Baxter."

Fred blinked. That had to be a made-up name.

"And if you must know a little more, I work for a firm in Chicago that makes religious calendars. Mostly for Methodists, although anybody can buy them. I do the art work and write the religious maxims for the calendar."

Fred nodded. That explained the ink-stained fingertips. "You mean a sort of tear calendar? Where you tear off a sheet for each day of the year?"

"Yes. I take a text from the Bible and then I write a little one paragraph homily based on the text."

Pa and Ma used to have a tear calendar. So. The woman's name had to be for real then. A person writing religious homilies would hardly lie. Fred let down a shoulder. "Well, glad to meet you, Miss Baxter." Fred turned to the attendant. "Okay, let's draw that map." Fred went over and stood tight against the light-blue wall, heels, butt, shoulderblades, and back of the head.

81

With a funny tortured smile the attendant took the chalk, and starting at one heel drew a white outline all the way around Fred down to the other heel. To trace over the top of Fred's head he had to rise on his toes. "There you are, Miss Baxter."

Fred stepped away. "Will that do?"

Miss Minerva Baxter examined the big human map. Finally she said, "Yes, that will be sufficient." She clutched her purse to her bosom. "Come, let's be on our way."

"Okay."

They stepped outside. She waved Fred to the driver's side of the car while she headed briskly for the passenger side. Fred tossed his suitcase in back on top of her things and got in.

He slipped under the steering wheel and was pleased to discover there was enough leg room. In most cars his knees were usually tight up against the steering wheel, and sometimes he had trouble shifting into reverse or low. It helped that the emergency brake was on the left or door side, almost under the dashboard. The dashboard was a fancy affair, nickel gauges for oil and gas and mileage all set tastefully into black sheet metal. He looked for the heat gauge; finally spotted it outside mounted on top of the black radiator cap. It resembled an old Egyptian sign for the sun, a circle resting on a flat bar. No red showed in the thermometer.

Miss Minerva watched him closely.

Fred noticed the ornamental insignia circling the horn in the center of the steering wheel. "Say, this is a Super Six Essex."

"Of course. I wanted a good car."

"Like I said, kind of old though."

"Well, I didn't want to buy a new car since I only wanted it long enough to get to my . . ." She bit her

82

tongue; then quickly added, "It was my thought to sell it when I arrived and so get my transportation free."

Fred didn't right away catch the pause. He glanced at the speedometer again. "Wow, only 21,000 on it. Unless of course they tampered with it."

"My brother told me to watch out for that and they assured me they hadn't tampered with it."

"I bet you got a bargain."

"We needn't go into that." She reset herself in the seat with a little hunching movement. "Well, let us be on our way."

Fred jiggled the stick shift to make sure the car was out of gear, turned the key. When the motor didn't catch hold right away, he pulled out the choke a careful quarter inch. The motor caught, roaring up a little, then slowly settling into a smooth purr. "Wow, what a motor."

Miss Minerva watched him.

Fred's eye next spotted a 3x5 card stuck to the windshield just in front of the steering wheel. It was what the woman was staring at earlier when she'd choked the motor to a stop. "What's that for?"

"Instructions on how to operate this vehicle."

"What do you need them for?" He read the neatly typed lines outloud.:

"1. Put gear shift in neutral position. Set choke. Push starter button.
2. Once engine is started, push in clutch, shift to low, let clutch out slowly. Accelerate.
3. When speedometer shows 15 miles an hour shift to intermediate. Same procedure as above.
4. When speedometer shows 25 miles an hour shift to high. Increase speed as needed.
5. To back up, push in clutch, shift to reverse, let out clutch slowly.

6. To park, turn off switch and pull up emergency brake."

There were more instructions on when to add oil, when to change oil, when to give the entire vehicle a grease job.

Miss Minerva said, "You see, I never drove a car before I bought this one."

Fred understood then why the poor woman had earlier come to a jerking stop, killing the motor. She was driving according to typed instructions, not out of easy habit. Further, to stop the car, she'd read the instructions in reverse order, from number 4 up through number 1. Fred stared at her. "How did you manage to drive out of Chicago in all that roaring traffic?"

"Nevermind. I'm here now and that's all that counts."

"Whew."

"Shall we get started?"

"Okay." Fred pushed in the clutch, shifted into low, let out the clutch slowly and smoothly. The old Essex rolled easily out of the filling station.

"So that's how you do it. I must learn to be that smooth too."

Fred shifted into second and headed the car north toward the schoolhouse and the water tower on the highest hill. "You mean to tell me those guys sold it to you without at least driving it around the block with you?"

"They said they were much too busy."

"The lousy bastards."

Miss Minerva winced. "Oh, dear, I do hope you're not going to turn out to be one of those men who swear."

Fred shifted to high and stepped on the footfeed. The powerful Super Six Essex motor climbed the hill easily.

The steering wheel responded to the slightest touch.

The sky over the brown brick high school and beyond over the black water tower was full of high blue illumination. It was as if the light-blue sky were raining down marvelous daylight and not the yellow sun. Fred pointed to the children playing on the swings and teeter-totters. "At least those kids are having a lot of fun."

"How can you be looking at them and be driving at the same time?"

"Driving comes easy for me."

The road turned left around the water tower and headed downhill toward some brush along a creek. The land continued to show deep fissures in all directions.

The paved road was as smooth as a swing. A junction showed up just beyond the creek bottom. Highway 83. A sign pointing north read: *Pierre, 32 miles.*

Gradually the road lifted again. Ahead lay an immense slope of earth, miles long and wide. More and more the dimensions of the country became fabulous, of a part with the brilliant skies.

As he drove, the back of his head continued to go over the woman next to him point for point. Probably about forty-five years old. No engagement ring or wedding band on the ringfinger of the left hand. Good full bosom. Well-shaped calves. Really a well-set up woman.

The Super Six motor soon warmed up and purred even more smoothly.

Fred cleared his throat. "Can I ask you a question?"

"Certainly."

"Are you married?"

"No, thank God."

"But you have a boyfriend?"

"No."

"Really?"

"No."

"Ever wish for one?"

"No, I never have."

Fred thought that unlikely. She was probably embittered over some love affair she'd had when young and was now pretending she'd never been interested in boys. Fred decided to change the subject. "You got relatives in Murdo then?"

"No, I haven't."

"I thought you said you were going as far as Murdo?"

She stared grimly ahead. "I hope you're not going to be one of those who's nosey."

"Sorry."

Draper coming up ahead was perched high on a hill. The little town looked like a tiny pincushion resting on a wide pillow. Its red water tower stuck out like a thimble mounted on several toothpicks.

Fred relaxed, slid down in the seat a little. The car ran easy. He drove it with one hand. He rested his left arm out of the open window.

The tar road abruptly changed to washboard gravel once more. The old Essex still drove easy.

"Don't you think you ought to drive with both hands on this rough stuff?" Miss Minerva asked.

"Maybe I should at that." Fred took hold of the steering wheel with both hands.

She looked at his big tanned hands appreciatively. "Maybe you're strong enough to drive with one hand, but I'm not."

"It's still a good idea to drive with both hands. I guess I was showing off a little. Hit a chuckhole and you can get thrown into the ditch driving with one hand."

Miss Minerva liked it that he'd agreed with her.

Fred's roving eye picked out a butte on the right. It had a white head and resembled an elongated footstool.

Miss Minerva said with a little smile, her first one,

86

"And now, may I ask where you are going?"

"Black Hills. Yellowstone."

"You have a job there?"

"No."

"What then?"

"I decided that before I'd take on a job I had to see the mountains."

"After you get to see Yellowstone, then what?"

"I've got a friend living in Belgrade, Montana. He's coming back through this way in a couple of weeks and I can ride with him home back to my pa's."

"What's this friend do? Rancher?"

"Ha. No, Don's a student. He graduated with me last June and this fall is going on to the seminary."

Miss Minerva's face lighted up. "He's going to become a minister?"

"That's right."

"Hmm." She reset herself in the seat. "So that's who your friends are. That speaks well for you."

"Thanks."

"And you, what are you going to be? A minister too?"

"Oh man no."

"Teacher then?"

"Not that either."

"Why not?"

"I took one look at the teachers I worked under in practice teaching and I knew. Most were dried up. Over particular. Teachers are overworked. It's really a thankless job."

"You're afraid of a little hard work?"

"Not at all. But I didn't want to be so overworked teaching that I wouldn't have any time left to write."

Miss Minerva considered him carefully. "So you want to write too."

Too?

87

"Do you have any of your writings with you?" she asked.

"No. I'm not much for writing when I'm on the go. I've got to hole up somewhere to write."

"Hmm. Well, I've got some of my things with me. Later on, remind me when we stop, that I give you some."

Fred could just see her stuff.

"I think it's lovely that you have the ambition to write. And I wish you success in it."

"Thanks."

From the tone of his voice she gathered he wasn't thinking the same thing she was. After several moments of reflection, she asked, "What sort of things do you write?"

Fred gave her question a turn or two through his head. He decided to be honest with her. "In college I wrote some poetry. It really wasn't much good. Too goody-goody and full of the silly search for what I called 'tesselated beauty.' But I did write one good piece of prose about a harvest scene." He didn't tell her that he'd also started a novel, some 90 pages worth, which he'd burned, because when a girl named Marion read it, she'd almost laughed her head off about the way he described a woman dressing in the morning.

"Prose."

"Yeh. Someday, maybe, I'll write a good novel."

Miss Minerva bounced in her seat. "Novels! Inventions of the devil."

"What about *The Scarlet Letter?*"

"That's a terrible book. Adultery! When I learned what it was about I almost threw it in the fire. That a minister should commit adultery."

"But Hawthorne?"

"I don't care if it's Shakespeare. That's not the kind

88

of thing people should read. Truly, it can be said of novels that the reading of them leads to the deterioration of the soul."

"You mean, much reading is a weariness of the flesh, don't you?"

"Verily, I say unto you, it is all vanity. A vanity of vanities."

Fred smiled sideways. "Yes, but the Bible also tells us that if you have a talent at something, it's wrong to bury it. And if a person has a talent to write good novels, why, it would be a crime not to. And it would be a further crime if people didn't read such novels."

After a pause, Miss Minerva said evenly, "I do hope you're not going to be one of those people who lusts after the fleshpots of Egypt."

Fred decided to drop the subject. Murdo had just come into view. It too lay on a wide pillow of a hill. It was a good-sized town. "Well, I guess here is where we part company."

"Murdo already?"

"That's right." As he spoke it suddenly hit Fred that she was going to be driving farther than Murdo, that she'd deliberately given him the name of the next big town so that in case he didn't work out as a driver she could dump him.

Miss Minerva stared ahead. Her left knee began to wiggle back and forth. There came from her the emanation that she was trying to figure out how to save face.

Fred decided to help her out. "Really too bad this is as far as you're going. Because I've enjoyed my ride with you."

"Well . . ." Her left knee moved faster. "I tell you, young man" — she quick grabbed her purse and pawed through it and came up with a sheet of paper with some writing on it — "I've just decided I won't stop here after

89

all." Her eyes rolled slightly. "If it is all right with you, we'll go on to Kadoka."

Fred kept a straight face. "Somebody you know there too?"

"Will you drive the car that far for me?"

"I'll be happy to, Miss Minerva."

She wasn't sure she liked it that he called her Miss Minerva. She hesitated a moment, then said, "Anyway, that's settled then. Good."

Fred kept a smile to himself. Actually she was going quite a ways west. Certainly all the way to the Black Hills. If he'd play along with her little game of pretending she was only going to the next big town, and if he could keep from offending her old maid sensibilities, by nightfall he'd be seeing his first mountains. A surge of joy poured into him, opening his nostrils, widening his eyes. Everything was going to be wonderful.

Fred slowed as they entered Murdo. The town was named after a famous pioneer cattleman, Murdo McKenzie. The houses weren't much different from those in Vivian. But the downtown was better kept up. Most stores had well-painted fronts. A half-dozen cars stood parked along the wide sidewalks. Fred counted four women and six children window-shopping.

Miss Minerva looked at the gas gauage. "We have enough for Kadoka, I see."

"More than plenty."

On the west edge of town, going down toward a creek, the gravel road quietly become smooth tar again.

Miss Minerva relaxed. "My, what a pleasure it is to ride on paved roads. That's where Chicago has it all over South Dakota."

Fred wasn't sure he wanted to pick that up.

The country became even more open and the horizons more distant. The grass to either side of the road was so utterly dead it lay faded beyond a pale gray. It was country that should never be plowed. The soil was of a kind that no matter how much rain fell it would never produce a decent crop of corn or grain. Bushes along the creeks told the story. They were stunted.

Far in the southwest hung the vague opalescent image of what appeared to be a butte. It had a dark top suggesting there might be a sprinkling of cedars on its crest. It looked a little like the ragged back of a tyrannosaur.

The little town of Okaton came up on the left. Except for curtains in some of the windows it too had a deserted look. The elevator along the railroad tracks was sandblasted down to the raw color of natural wood, especially the top half.

Fred thought of Special Face. He wondered where she might be, what she might be doing right that minute. Probably sitting in a lawn chair in her backyard reading a good book. A sprinkler would be on, whistling out water in varying vaporous umbrellas, and the grass around her would be green. There'd be the smell of a freshly mowed lawn, of oozing grass sap. Only trouble was, Special Face wouldn't in turn be thinking of him. She'd be thinking of the other fellow.

Fred almost let out a groan, outloud, when he remembered the one time Special Face had let him make a little time with her.

. . . . The Pierian Club, of which he'd been miraculously elected president, was having its annual picnic on a sandy beach along Lake Michigan, near Muskegon. As president, he'd finally talked her into a date. They rode with Red Hekman, a rich man's son. Young Hekman had suggested they double-date in his dad's Cadillac. Fred wasn't sure if Special Face went

91

along with him because she liked riding in style in a Cadillac or because he'd begged her so hard for the date.

On the way home, sitting together in the back seat, zooming along as though in dream, she touched him on the hand. "Feike," she whispered, "if you want to you may."

His brain lit up like a telephone switchboard after a tornado. "You mean?"

"Yes. You've been telling me to give you a chance, that if we were to touch, something magical might happen between us."

"Oh, yes. That." For a second he'd thought she meant they should do it, copulate, on the back seat of the Cadillac, and he hadn't thought she'd ever have such thoughts, and it stunned him to think it.

She touched him again. "Feike?" She had a way of saying his nickname that hinted of another word, the one lying submerged just beneath it. "Feike?"

"Yes?"

"If you want to?"

He groaned, and with yet another moan all the way out of his bones, turned ever so slightly and slipped his arms around her, and held her up off the seat, a little light slim bunny, not quite crushing her, holding her so that he took the bumps of the pavement for her by making a swing of his arms. But he was too paralyzed with love to make love to her.

After the long long ride back to Grand Rapids, it was soon all to apparent that she'd lost interest in him. He hadn't taken advantage of her the one time she was willing, press in and make ardent love . . . .

Fred drove the old Essex steadily for Miss Baxter across South Dakota.

92

He thought of Helen of Troy and the war she'd caused. He could just see her. She'd look a little like his Special Face, lightgold hair, fine as spider threads, flowing in pongee folds to her shoulders as she walked. She too would stride so erect she'd appear to be leaning back a little, as though her legs were outrunning the rest of her. For so tiny a thing she'd be as brave as a mink. Because it would take a lot of bravery to run away from a warrior like Menelaus and live with Paris.

He thought of yet another Special Face, the one at Calvin who'd dated him for the annual Junior-Senior banquet, because it was Leap Year.

. . . . Fred knew Special Face One wouldn't ask him for a date since she'd be asking her new boy friend. In fact Fred was sure he was going to be overlooked for the party. Who'd ask him? Girls thought him much too tall to date. Too much of freak.

But one evening he was called to the phone out in the Dorm hallway. Fred wondered who could be calling him. He never got calls.

Some of the boys jeered him as he walked past them in the lobby. "Bet a buck it's Miss Fatty calling you." Miss Fatty was a junior. She was plump and a little too forward for the boys.

Fred squeezed himself into the phone booth, closed the narrow folding doors. "Yes?"

"Frederick Feikema?"

"Yes?"

The girl on the line gave her name. It was Special Face Two. She was from one of the more exclusive families in town. She was dark where Special Face One was light. And she too was a small slim thing. My God, what did she see in him? He was at least a foot and a half taller than she. And he came from a farm family.

93

She had to be spoofing him.

"Oh, yes. What can I do for you?" he said politely.

There was a slight pause, then she said, "I was hoping no one'd asked you for a date to the Junior-Senior party." There it was.

"No," he said, "no one has."

"Oh, good. Because I'd like to take you. If I may."

Fred slowly turned stiff in the tight phone booth. There wasn't a hint of a spoof in her voice. She meant it. Holy suffering gonads. He didn't love her, would probably never love her, but she was the catch on the campus. "Yes." Then Fred added one of Special Face One's pet phrases. "I'd like that."

"Good. I'll call for you around six o'clock. Will that be all right?"

"Yes. That'll be fine."

"Good. Be seeing you. Bye."

The boys in the Dorm right away knew someone had asked him for a date. For several days they tried to pry it out of him. Fred only smiled and pretended it was nothing to get excited about.

On the night of the party, at six o'clock, the boys were all in the lobby when Special Face Two rode up in a black limousine. The chauffeur got out and came up the front steps and called for Fred. Wow. The taunters fell silent. At the same time their eyes were filled with grudging admiration.

The evening became an especial success when, after the party, Special Face Two instructed the chauffeur to drive around Reeds Lake several times. "Because," she said, "I want to know you, Frederick."

She asked him about his family, his friends back home, his dead mother, his dreams, did he go to church Sundays, and even asked him about Special Face One. One moment Fred was bursting with pride, the next moment felt collapsed inside because he knew that no matter what they might do together he'd never be able to turn himself around, reset his cells to the pull of another magnetic pole, and love Special Face Two . . . .

"You do go to church Sundays, don't you?"
Fred almost jumped out of his skin. His soul snapped back from Grand Rapids to Miss Minerva Baxter's Super Six Essex. Ye gods, it was as if the forty-five year old spinster sitting next to him had picked his brain for those two words "church Sundays."
"Or aren't you really much of a church-goer?"
"Oh, I go to my father's church all right."
"You mentioned you were Frisian-Dutch. Do you go to the Dutch Reformed Church?"
"Dutch Christian Reformed."
"Oh," she said, pleased. "They're strict!"
"They sure are."
"Don't you like your church?"
Fred pursed his lips. "Oh, there are a lot of fine people in it. But the church and I don't see eye to eye on some things."
"Such as?"
Fred resented the question. She'd burst in on some choice private rememberings. The impulse to be a bit cruel with her took him over for the moment. "Well, the church is dead wrong about sex. God would never have given us a powerful sex drive and made it so pleasurable if he didn't think it was all right. I don't think He ever intended that we should think of sex as sinful."

Miss Minerva gave herself a violent hunching motion beside him. Her face remained, composed, however, and her voice quietly pedagogical. "What about the Seventh Commandment?"

"That's about adultery. I'm talking about sex between two people who love each other. Between a man and a wife who love each other very much."

"Sex! Sex! All you young people think of nowadays is sex. You're sex-besotted." Her whole mouth fell back into a set expression, as though she were about to yell out of an old agony. They'd hit on the one subject on which she was extremely touchy.

"Don't you believe in touching at all then?"

"Heavens, no. My father never touched me. Nor my mother, as far as that goes. Nor did my brother in Boise. We just never did that."

"Well, my family was a family of touchers. My mother was always touching us boys. And Pa was too. Somebody's hand was always on us. Loving and kind."

"Och! how awful. I just can't stand to have anybody touch me."

Stamford drifted by. One building housed all the business places: general store, post office, filling station. A single red gas pump stood out front. There were two houses in back. The walk to the best house was lined with collapsed geraniums.

Miss Minerva gave herself another hunching motion, moving away from him as far as she could. "Now I am glad I made that filling station boy draw an outline of you on his wall. Because I can already see that you have it in you to be a potential sex fiend."

"Oh, come now, Miss Minerva."

"It's true!"

"Really, now. I haven't even remotely made the slightest move toward you. Not even one fingertip."

"Ohh but I know your kind."

Fred decided she'd probably been rushed by some brute of a fellow. "Listen, Miss Minerva, a lot of us fellows are still idealistic, still considerate. I know that I for one am one of those. I couldn't rape you anymore

96

than the man in the moon could."

"I don't believe you."

"Well, Miss Minerva, it goes like this. And now I'm going to have to say something you won't like. To rape a woman you have to have an erection."

Miss Minerva almost shot up through the roof of her Super Six Essex. "Erection! Why . . .!" She began to gasp like a fish thrown up on shore. "Why Mister Feikema! I forbid you to use such dirty words in my car."

"Nevertheless, there has to be an erection for there to be intromission. And I know. I'm one of those guys who'd go impotent if he'd try rushing a girl who didn't like him. It just isn't in me to be that kind of brute."

"Och! I can hardly believe you. You're just as bad as the rest of them. Because where did you learn all such talk? Disgusting."

"On the farm, Miss Minerva. Chickens, pigs, cows, horses. You see it all around you every day. Especially in the spring."

"But I don't believe that about some men not being able to."

"Why, Miss Minerva, you even see impotence, or disinterest, in the animal kingdom."

"Ho, ho."

It happened that off on their right a black bull stood alone on a knoll. The bull appeared to be dejected, head lowered, as if he were the last of his kind in all of that dry country.

Fred pointed. "There's probably one of them right now. A bachelor bull."

"You mean gentleman cow."

Fred stared at her. The old Essex motor purred underfoot. "Ha. That's what my Kathryn calls 'em."

"You mean the lady who wrote the letter I read?"

97

"Exactly."

Miss Minerva was somewhat mollified. "Well, I can see where despite your being a man, you come of good people."

"Oh for godsakes. Listen, Pa often used to . . . We once had an old bull named Tom. Pa thought him the best he ever had. Active? Man! But yet there'd always be one cow he'd never cover. As if he didn't care for her."

"I don't believe it. I just don't believe it."

"True though. In fact, Pa usually got rid of the cow that Tom wouldn't cover. Pa said she had to be no good if Tom didn't care for her. Tom knew."

"Thomas the gentleman cow, you mean."

Fred threw up his hands in exasperation; quickly resettled them on the steering wheel.

Belvidere with its few scattered buildings up on an airy slope came toward them like an apparition. A woman in the last house on the west end of town was hanging out her wash.

The road turned to washboard gravel again.

Miss Minerva, deep in thought, had more to say. "Well, maybe there are those kind of men. Jesus was like that."

"You mean Jesus was a gentleman cow?"

"No no!" she snapped. "Don't be sacrilegious. I mean, he was the kind of man who would be most considerate of a woman."

Fred nodded with a little smile. "Jesus could hardly be accused of rape."

Miss Minerva fronted him with a hard brown look. "You know, there's a cynical air about you that I don't like."

"Can't you take a joke?"

"Not when it comes to my Savior Jesus Christ."

"Now now, I'm sure that the Good Lord has a sense

of humor."

"As a Methodist I don't like it."

"All right."

"You know, really, you're a bit uppity for one who's getting a free ride. I should ask you to get out. And let you walk the rest of the way to Kadoka."

"It's up to you."

They rode a ways before she spoke again. "Where do you get all that self-confidence? And get it so young?"

Fred wheeled the car expertly around an old chuckhole. "Maybe from my father. My father was a hero. He used to say that no matter what happened, he always tried to land on his feet leaning forward and already on the run."

"Hitchhiking like this, when you're waiting for a ride, don't you ever get that lost feeling that the whole world has deserted you?"

"No. I usually think that pretty soon something wonderful is going to happen."

"Don't you ever worry about who might pick you up next? That he might turn out to be a murderer?"

"Or a rapist?" Possibly a woman?"

Her mouth once again fell into that set expression as though she were about to yell out of an old ache. "A woman can't rape a man!"

"Ha. That's a great thought. Why not? She can seduce him, can't she?"

"But she can't . . . Ohch, how is it that we always keep falling into these wretched shameful conversations. You really have it on the brain, haven't you?"

"Wait a minute. I'm not the one who's the first to think evil of other people. You are." Fred slapped the steering wheel. "Ha. The trouble with me is, I'm a softie. I'm much too trusting."

She sat chewing her lips.

99

Fred let down a shoulder. He decided to tell her a little how it felt, really, to be a hitchhiker. "Actually, you know, a hitchhiker is kind of an old time minnesinger. He entertains the travelers he catches rides with. A car comes along and stops and gives him a lift. The hitchhiker repays the kind driver with the tale of his life. He sings for his ride so to speak. I caught a lot of rides going to Calvin for four years and I noticed after a while that I got better and better at telling my life story. Hitchhikers get to be excellent story tellers. They're constantly redoing their story to suit the audience's taste."

Miss Minerva sniffed. "Weren't the minnesingers really gay troubadors who went from town to town singing love songs to the maidens to win them over to their hedonistic way of life?"

Fred crooked his head. She had a point there.

The black tower of Kadoka poked up over the next rise. It was like a great stovehat on a tall man, with the tall man slowly getting to his feet. As they crested the next hogback the whole town came into view. It was surprisingly good-looking: three well-kept tourist camps, wide clean streets, new storefronts, many freshly painted homes.

Fred slowed for a cross road. He looked at the gas gauge. "This car sure don't eat much gas." Then he added, knowing that in a moment Miss Minerva would have to tell him she wasn't really going to stop in Kadoka, "We can easy go on to Wall before getting gas."

Miss Minerva's knee began to wiggle again. She'd forgotten that their arrangement was for him to drive on a town-to-town basis. Her eyes appeared to sink back under her forehead.

Fred stepped on the brake and angled over onto the

100

shoulder of the road. "Well, if I'm going to get out, it'd better be right here, before you go into town."

"Wait. I mean, I . . ." Then she mustered up courage and spoke her mind. "After all, this is my car, and I didn't know you from Adam when I first picked you up, and I guess I have the right to make sure of you before telling you just how far I'm going. So drive on."

Fred let up on the brake and swung back into his lane again. "Good. And now, lady, is there any harm in your telling me exactly where you're going? I told you everything about where I'm going."

She didn't quite look him in the eye. "I'm going to the Black Hills."

"Great! This is going to turn out to be a wonderful long ride after all."

"Yes." She hunched herself about in the seat. "Rapid City, that's where . . . I'll go."

"What'd you come out west for?"

"See my brother. And once I get there I'm going to sell this car. If I can get my money back I'll have my transportation free. Good cars are scarce out there and he thought I could easy sell it. Maybe even for a profit."

"Then you're not going back to Chicago?"

She fell silent once more.

He drove a couple of more miles, when all of a sudden he saw the ragged back of a tyrannosaur again. "Hey," he exclaimed mildly. He spotted a sign ahead where the road forked. One arrow pointed north: *Wall, 30 miles.* Another arrow pointed straight ahead: *Badlands, 20 miles.* "Hey, that I want to see." He pulled up sharply on the side of the road.

Miss Minerva shrank away from him as far as she could get, pressing against the door. "Ohh, I suppose now it begins," she wailed.

"I've heard so much about the Badlands that I really

101

ought to see them. Especially since Grampa once home-steaded in them somewhere." Then Fred noticed Miss Minerva. "What?"

"You men!" she squeaked. "Leading me on all this time, letting me think you were a nice young man, when all along all you were interested in was in getting me alone in this godforsaken place."

"Good God."

"You had it in mind all along that you were going to rape me. And beat me up for my money."

Fred stared at her in disbelief. "Holy suffering Peter. Why, it really is you who's got sex on the brain all the time."

"You aren't stopping here then to molest me?"

"Of course not. Like I said, I just now remembered that Grampa homesteaded out here once. Besides, I hear the Badlands are beautiful. Marvelous. Wonderful. A great sight to see."

"Oh."

Fred continued to look at her in disgust. "The way you throw those words around, murder, rape, molest . . . what do you really know about them?"

She withdrew from the door and sat up very straight. "Not so fast now, young man. After all, I really was at your mercy, you know. And you are terribly big. I wouldn't have much chance against you with those big hands of yours."

Fred let out a huge sigh. "Look. You're a real nice lady. Very much like my Aunt Kathryn. But just like her, you'd be the last person on earth I'd want to go spooning with. Like Pa's bull Tom being choosey. Besides, you're much too old for me. Begging your pardon, but you are."

Miss Minerva gave him a torn look.

"Well, not that we've got that settled, how about it,

102

shall we take that tour through the Badlands? It's right on the way to the Black Hills." Fred looked up through the windshield. "The sun is still pretty high in the sky." He dug out his Standard Oil map of South Dakota. He traced the road for her with a long forefinger. "See? Instead of sticking to 16 and going north here, we could go straight south a ways down to Interior, and then once again head west and follow the north rim of the Badlands almost all the way to Wall."

Grudgingly she looked at the map. "Suppose my car breaks down in there?"

"This Super Six Essex? Never."

"Well, I had planned on seeing some of the sights."

Fred did some calculating. "It shouldn't be more than about fifteen miles out of the way."

"And I suppose it is educational."

"My friend Don took it once and he says the U.S. Government has built a nice road through it."

Miss Minerva finally nodded. "All right, we shall see it. Drive on, young man."

Fred craved a smoke. It had been hours since his last one back in Vivian.

"Something the matter?"

"Nope." Fred put the car in gear. "Here goes nothing." They crossed the corner and headed west. They were about to see a great thing.

The gravel road was rough. Five miles farther along the land dropped away on their left, and a whole valley full of rampant tyrannosaurs opened to view.

Fred slowed down. "Look at that. It's hard to believe."

Miss Minerva wasn't sure she liked it.

Then the opening in the land closed and once again they rode on flat burnt land.

"Wasn't that something."

103

She frowned to herself. "It's hard to figure out what the Good Lord had in mind creating such desolation. But He must've had a purpose in mind."

"His purpose was probably to show us that sometimes He can be an artist too."

"God is a God of justice, not of art."

"That's where I differ with you again. Besides, true full justice includes art."

The road turned left, zigzagged several times, then once again the land on their left dropped away. Before them lay a confusion of weird beautiful shapes, natural pyramids, ghostly peaks, tottering pinnacles. Delicate pink and cream and rose and chalk-white colors set off the various strata. The road wound down through it all, first right and then left, at last headed for a one-story government building.

Fred stopped the car beside a sign. Both he and Miss Minerva stared up through the windshield to read the legend. It told how an ancient stream had once flowed through that very spot some 23 million years ago. The stream had left gravel and coarse sand behind. Some of the gravel later formed into a conglomerate called sandstone. The upper third of most cliffs and most of the taller spires were partly volcanic ash. It accounted for the strange luminescent purple tinting.

Someone had tacked a notice on the bottom of the sign warning that there might be an occasional prairie rattlesnake sunning itself on the sand. "Stay on the trail and stay alert."

Fred could still feel the chill of that rattler sleeping against him under his red blanket. "Great country, but I sure don't like rattlers."

Miss Minerva didn't much like rattlers either. "Let's move on. I'd like to get to Rapid before dark."

Fred swung the old Essex over onto the road. The

gravel road went south a ways, then swung west. They passed one sharp-edged yellowgold gully after another. The road wound through a magic land of natural minarets and castles and fortress walls. Pink and ochre and yellow lay in level parallels in all directions.

Miss Minerva couldn't stand it after a while. She lowered her eyes and picked at a thread in her skirt.

Fred drove slowly through the scenery. The different angles and serrated projections hit him like sharply struck notes on a piano. The oranges and yellows and ochres kept blending off into each other in the most delicate of shadings, reminding him of Fritz Kreisler playing *Liebestraum* on the violin. He had to fight off the impulse to get out of the car and jump up and down.

Fred finally spotted a parking area ahead and made up his mind. He drove into the parking lot and stopped the car and turned to Miss Minerva. "I don't know about you, lady, but I've just got to get out and see this close up. Okay?"

Miss Minerva continued to pick at a thread over her knee.

"It's wrong to rush past such marvels. I've got to walk into it a ways. Touch it."

She sat like a hen that'd spotted a hawk overhead and was making herself as small as possible.

"I'll be back in a jiff." He slipped out and closed the door behind him.

There were several other cars in the parking area, with license plates from distant states: New York, Massachusetts, Oregon, California. The cars were empty, everybody having scattered out along the winding path into the canyon.

The sandy clay path crackled under his oxfords. The sound of it was like walking on kernels of corn left scattered on a cement feeding platform. The path curved

105

left down through a patch of juniper. Dusty purplish berries studded every branch. The sweetish odor rising from the juniper reminded him of a shaving lotion.

Clusters of stunted cottonwoods grew in the moist turns. The cottonwood leaves had brilliant red stems. Dark green rubber rabbitbush grew in the deeper reaches of the canyon. Tiny birds cast flitting shadows in the thicker bushes.

Fred spotted red berries in some bushes with silver leaves. That had to be the buffalo berry Grampa Feike used to talk about. It made a delicious clear jelly.

There were voices up ahead, excited children clambering up the slopes of the various downslumps, and nervous parents warning them to be careful. Mingled with it all were the raucous complaints of several black-and-white magpies. The magpie was a daring bird and didn't move until one was almost upon it. Then it jumped up, squawking loudly, appearing to use its long black drooping tail to give itself a pushoff.

The path wound around an immense monument-like pillar. The pillar thinned as it rose upward, until at its very tip it fluted out to a flat crest. Hundreds of strata hung outlined in the pillar, all the shadings possible between pink and gold.

Around yet another corner Fred came upon a perfectly sculptured candelabrum. It was so delicately balanced on a slender stem that but a touch of a finger would send it crashing to earth.

He smelled something dead. Rabbit? He moved into a side arroyo and the smell became stronger. A few steps more he saw it. A dead coyote. Someone had shot it. Two small-headed black turkey vultures were tugging away at its burst bowels. Shadows touched Fred and looking up he spotted two more vultures circling overhead, tiny heads peering down.

106

Fred glanced at his wristwatch. Four bells. He'd better get back.

Just as he turned the corner past the delicately balanced candelabrum, he noticed a bone sticking out of a yellow-pink wall at about eye level. The bone was huge, as big as a stovepipe. That had to be the thighbone of a dinosaur. He reached out and touched it. It felt dry and very old. It looked like the bone he'd once seen in the Field Museum in Chicago. With a fingernail Fred scratched the surface of the bone. It broke open easily, exposing a honeycomb structure.

Fred's heart beat big and slow and hard. His vision was jarred with each pulse. He had the feeling that the top of his head had opened up like a huge coneflower, that his brain had become a great eye looking straight up into angel country. His nostrils felt as big as barrels.

Ecstasy. He was having the brain explosion of a Chaucer or a Van Gogh. It was how they felt when they were at the top of their bent.

Vaguely a voice penetrated his euphoria. Miss Minerva.

"Mister Feikema? Mister Feikema?" There was a note of concern in her voice. Ah. She was beginning to like having him around.

He trudged back, slowly. He hated to leave the yellow wound. The falling sunlight fell bright on the golden erosion. The serrated knife edges of the buttes shimmered like they might be the saffron flames of a burning strawpile.

Miss Minerva was standing outside the car when he turned up the last winding curve. She was upset. Her fingers twitched. "I was sure you'd gone and hurt yourself. Slipped and fell somewhere."

Fred let himself down reluctantly. "No."

"You were gone so long."

107

"You should have come with me."

"Well, perhaps I should have. But I'm not much for the marvels of nature."

"I'm still driving?"

"Of course." Fingers still twisting, she went around to her side of the car. "You're a good driver."

He got in and settled himself comfortably behind the wheel. He lifted the creases of his trousers free of his sweating limbs. "Thanks. And thank you too for waiting here."

"Don't mention it."

They climbed the road up onto the north wall of the Badlands and then followed it for several miles. Again and again the land opened up into deep holes and canyons and leached out valleys. No two views were the same.

When the road turned north, the earth filled up behind them and the sandstone tyrannosaurs and lovely tottering turrets vanished. They became ghosts in memory.

They got gas in Wall and drove on west.

Highway 16 speered down into the Cheyenne River valley. Waxy yucca studded the upper slopes of the breaks. Cottonwoods stippled the curving bottoms.

They passed through Wasta. They followed a very rough washboard highway up onto a plateau, raising a light-yellow plume of following dust which slowly wisped off to the north.

They passed through New Underwood with its few drab buildings and towering grain elevators. The bed of nearby Box Elder Creek was dry.

They'd driven in silence for some time, when Fred gradually became aware of a dark shadow on the horizon ahead. He leaned forward over the steering wheel for a closer look. "That's got to be a cloud of

108

some kind."

Miss Minerva looked too. "Yes."

One eye on the road, Fred watched the cloud come toward them. The upper fan of it quickly obscured the sun while the lower part of it became a considerable cumulus cloud. Then, as he watched, veils began to descend out of the dark bottom of the cloud. The veils hung slanting off to the north. "That's rain falling."

"How do you know?"

"Back home that's the way a cloud looks when it starts to rain."

"Maybe that means the end of the drouth."

Fred shook his head. "No. Not heavy enough. Didn't build up enough."

Both watched the cloud race toward them. It appeared to climb the sky. The veils beneath thinned, wavered, and like a series of horsetails flourished off to the north.

"Man, is that cloud high," Fred said to himself. "Back home such a cloud would come in with its black butt almost dragging on the ground."

Miss Minerva nodded. "It is a strange cloud at that. It's almost like an apparition."

The fan of the cloud above them split and gradually assumed the form of wings. Its blackness turned to a gray sheen.

"Looks like an old time Indian thunderbird."

Miss Minerva didn't like hearing about such things. "Heathen nonsense."

Fred smiled at her. "That's what the Sioux probably say about our Holy Ghost."

"That's different. We have the Bible for proof that there is a Holy Ghost."

"Did you ever see the Holy Ghost?"

Miss Minerva threw him a hurt look and then turned

109

to watch the fenceposts flash by.

The vaporous thunderbird continued to lift over them, trailing many thin legs. One of the longer thin legs came dragging straight toward them down the gravel highway. In another moment a dozen huge raindrops sprettled noisily all over the windshield. And then, the next moment, the high cloud was behind them.

Fred opened the window a crack on his side. Instantly there was a smell as of freshly cut sunflowers in the car. "Even if it was only a sprinkle, what a great smell it is when rain falls on dry grass." Fred drove on a few miles. "That's the trouble with rain in this West River Country. The clouds start out pretty good, but then all too soon they dry up and blow over."

The sun slowly settled in the west, soon was almost directly in their eyes. It was while he was trying to adjust a creaky visor above the windshield that Fred spotted a rising dark bulk far over the land dead ahead. "Hey, that's got to be the Black Hills."

Miss Minerva looked too. Again a look of resistance came into her eyes.

The blue-shouldered Hills kept rising in front of them. A small mountain range appeared to be making before their very eyes.

Fred said, "I'd always imagined the mountains to look like the Newton Hills back home . . . only quadrupled. With some sharp points on them covered with snow. But that's not it either. Mountains are completely different from what I thought they'd be."

"Well, as for me, never having seen them, I have no wish to know."

Presently Fred began to make out separate slopes and valleys. Every bulge was covered with dark evergreens. With the sun about to set behind them, he understood why they were called the Black Hills. The long purple afternoon shadows did it. It was hardly surprising that the Indians considered the dark high places their holy land. And it was also hardly surprising that the white man spoke of the Hills as a magic place in which to take a vacation.

The old Super Six Essex climbed and then crested a long slope of foothills. It made the sun hold for a moment above the Hills. Then the car descended the slope and the sun sank abruptly behind the Hills. Dusk spread toward them like a pushing purple fog. Fred turned on the car lights. At about the same time the lights of Rapid City appeared below them.

Miss Minerva became all business. "I want you to stop at the first stoplight. That's where I'm going to turn off."

Fred was a little startled. "Well, I guess then that's where I'll have to get out."

"Yes."

"Miss Baxter, you've been awfully nice to let me ride this far with you. You've given me a great lift."

"Don't mention it." There was an air about her as though she were making a point of being extra firm with him to make sure she wasn't going to relent and let him drive some more.

Traffic was heavy. Tourists were arriving. Local people were just then heading home for supper.

Fred negotiated his way to the first stop sign and pulled up beside a newsstand. "Well, here we are." He gave her a warm look. "Once again, Miss Baxter, it was lovely of you to let me ride this far."

"Thank you for driving for me."

Fred stepped out on his side and reached in back for his suitcase. "You sure you'll be all right in the city here?" His eyes flicked a look at the card of driving in-

111

structions stuck up on the windshield.

"I'll be fine." Miss Minerva slid over under the wheel."

"All right then." Fred stepped around behind the car and up on the curb. He stopped a moment beside the newsstand to make sure she got off all right.

Miss Minerva steeled herself into looking at the instruction sheet; pushed out her chin; and then, shifting, with a wild lurch zoomed off in low into the moving lights of the traffic.

Fred watched her go. "What a dame." He sighed, shifting the suitcase to his other hand. "I wish her luck. But God save me from any more like her. Because I don't think even old Casanova would have had a chance with her. If she were Eve, she'd be wearing the lobe of a pricklepear cactus instead of a fig leaf."

Fred walked until he came to the second stoplight. A Standard Oil filling station twinkled on the far corner. Fred strode over and was about to ask the operator if he could stand there and thumb for a ride, when a young redhead in a yellow roadster pulled up beside him brakes screeching.

"Want a lift?"

"Where you going?" Fred asked warily.

"Spearfish."

Fred went over a mental map of the Black Hills. "That's still 16, isn't it?"

"All the way."

Fred got in, throwing his suitcase in back.

The redhead let out the clutch in low, revved up the motor until they were going 30 miles an hour, then shifted directly into high gear. In a moment they were going 50 miles an hour. A minute later they were out in open country.

The Black Hills loomed up on their left like the great

112

shoulders of a herd of buffalo bulls crowded together. Open prairie spread away on their right for miles. Some light from the west still pushed over the high Hills, falling upon the prairies in slanting shafts of rust.

As the road curled and turned, the headlights of the yellow roadster shifted from one side to the other, illuminating a single home, a boulder, a pimple-like red hill, a flat red pasture, a rising slope toward a butte.

Fred thought he spotted some oddly cut logs in the rusty light.

The redhead caught his look. "Petrified trees."

Fred watched them go by in wonder.

"If we had time I'd let you have a look." The fellow had unruly red hair and thick sideburns. "There are a lot of things to look at along this road. Up ahead is Wonderland Cave. Then Crystal Cave."

"What's the rush?"

"I got a date with a hot freshie up at the State Teachers College."

The redhead's face was rough and pitted with blackheads. Fred wondered how any girl could go for a fellow with such terrible skin. Did she avoid touching that part of him when they kissed? Just as someday some girl would have to overlook his own defect, his damned height?

"Yep," the fellow said, "I don't see what she sees in me. But so long as it lasts I'm not asking any questions."

It made Fred smile. First he'd caught a ride with a cold pickle; then with a hotshot.

It was eight o'clock when the redhead pulled up beside a camping grounds on the outskirts of Spearfish.

Fred got out. "Thanks for the ride."

"Don't mention it." The redhead goosed his motor. "Tell you, the guy running this camp has a good heart. Pretend you're hard up and he'll give you a cot free in one of his tents." The redhead glanced at the gold letter on Fred's red sweater. "Especially since he has a boy in college."

"Thanks."

The redhead waved and was off.

Fred stood a moment alongside the road to collect himself. He looked up at the stars, glanced up at the towering Hills to the south, combed back his hair with his fingers, and then, taking a deep breath, headed for a neat white shack marked Office in the camping grounds. A sharp light shone above the door. Behind the one-story shack were two rows of wooden cabins, and still farther back, into the edge of a considerable forest, stood two rows of canvas tents. Cars were parked one by one next to the cabins. A haze of dust wavered across the bright light.

Fred entered the office. It was neat inside too.

A tall bowed proprietor looked up. "Yes?"

"You wouldn't happen to have a spare cot for mother's wandering boy tonight, would you?"

The proprietor studied Fred with sad eyes. "I won't know until later. Cars will keep dropping in for another couple of hours yet."

"Until how late you think?"

"Oh, around twelve."

"That long."

The proprietor gave Fred another look. "Tell you what. Hang around for a while and we'll see what happens. You can always roll up in a blanket in my woods back there."

"What about snakes?"

"Snakes don't like it this high up."

"Is there a restaurant nearby?"

"No, not for half a mile." The proprietor looked around at a stove behind him. "Tell you what. In a

114

minute I'm gonna make myself a hamburger. I'll throw an extra one on for you."

"How much?"

"What else but a dime?"

"Good."

The proprietor pointed to a chair by the window. "Take a load off your feet. Might as well make yourself t'home while you can."

Fred sat around for a half hour before the hamburgers were ready. Tourists kept dropping in to interrupt the proprietor's work at the stove. The hamburgers were thick with meat. The proprietor also set out a piece of thick apple pie and a cup of good black coffee with cream and sugar.

Fred dug out the dollar bill he had in his billfold and placed it on the makeshift counter.

The proprietor looked at it a moment. "Why don't you hang onto that greenboy until we see how many cots I got left. Later on maybe I can throw it all in for a buck."

"Fine."

Fred sat patiently in the tight little office. He hated waiting. He'd hated standing in line at Calvin on Admissions Day. He'd hated waiting in line in front of a movie. It was like handing over one's brains for a while.

He got out his map of Wyoming and studied it. Tomorrow he'd be headed into that storied country. Highway 16 crossed the Big Horn Mountains all the way to Worland. From there he'd have to take 20 to Yellowstone.

He next got out Whitman from his suitcase and read him for a while. But the light proved to be too dim, and presently, eyes watering, he put Whitman away.

Not wanting to pass the day without some kind of mind improvement, Fred got out his little black wordbook. He worked his way through two pages, savoring and studying each word carefully. Dilatory. Aeolian. Shaman. Benefactrix. Rattail file.

He tried to recall if he'd heard any interesting new words lately that he could add to the list. But the geologist hadn't used any that he could think of. Nor had Miss Minerva. Nor had Beeford the hobo. Nor playwright Rivers and his wife. Too bad. The day was going to pass without a new word found.

He felt a call to nature. He asked the lanky proprietor, "My suitcase will be safe here, won't it, while I go take a look at the stars?"

"Sure. The privy's around behind here."

Fred stepped outside. He couldn't stand the reek of old human dung. Instead of using the privy he wandered out into the dark forest a ways and selected an appropriate tree.

He stood a while in silence. A breeze stirred the tops of the ponderosa pine. Each tree spoke straight up toward the stars. Green needles threshed lightly. It was as though ghosts were passing through the fringe of a beaded curtain. The sound was aeolian.

He smiled a little to himself. It pleased him that he'd casually used one of the words he'd just finished studying.

A coyote howled out in the open country to the north. It was answered angrily by a dog from a nearby house.

There was a pervasive smell of fish on the air. No doubt there were fish in Spearfish Creek but they'd hardly give off that much of an odor.

Coming back to the office, he asked, "What's that heavy fish smell around here?"

"There's a U.S. Fish Hatchery at the foot of the canyon back there."

"It comes in pretty strong."

116

"We're used to it and never notice it."

"How are we doing with that tent?"

The proprietor thought to himself a moment. "Oh, heck, at the rate the tourists have been dropping in tonight, I'll never fill them all. Why don't you just take the end one out there, way out under the trees." The proprietor opened a storage box. "I've got no sheets for you, but I do have this." He tossed Fred a pillow. "That'll be a buck."

Fred dug out the dollar bill from his billfold.

"See you in the morning, son."

Carrying his suitcase Fred followed a dusty path out to the last tent. The tent had been set on the floor of the forest. Fred ducked inside. The tight canvas place was full of the odor of sweet crushed pine needles.

He lit a match. There were two folding cots, one against each wall with a path in between. He selected the one on the right. He liked to sleep on his right side. He waved out the match, and stuffed the burnt end of it deep into the soil underfoot. He kicked off his shoes, removed his trousers and sweater and tie and shirt, and getting out his red blanket, settled himself over the flimsy canvas cot. The cot turned out to be surprisingly stable once he'd settled on it. It was a little short and Fred as usual had to sleep with his feet sticking out over the end.

Then he remembered he'd better dig out some of the money he had in his shoe. He'd need it the next day. He reached for his oxford in the dark, and with careful fingers fished out a dollar bill, putting five back. A little curious, he gave the bill a sniff. It smelled a little of old socks. He stuffed the dollar bill in his billfold.

There was water running somewhere, a little stream trickling over mossy rocks. The trickling sound was cheerful.

117

Fred thought of That Special Face he'd lost; and then, to the sweet murmur of the trickling water, fell sound asleep.

VI

He awoke with a start at dawn. He sat up so quickly he almost tipped the cot over. It took him a moment to figure out where he was. Then he heard the sweet sound of the little trickling stream and remembered.

He got up and poked his head out through the tent flaps. Nobody in the next tents. He stepped outside in his underwear and had a look around. He took a deep breath of the ponderosa pine aroma and the high air of the Black Hills. He stretched himself, rising on his toes in sheer animal satisfaction.

He went back into his tent and dressed. To quell his hunger he got out his makings and had himself a cigarette. He stuffed out the matchhead deep into the raw red earth under the pine duff. He sat on the edge of the cot carefully smoking so as not to drop any live ashes on the pine needles. There were No Smoking signs everywhere in the Hills and he had to be careful. But the smoke didn't taste good before breakfast. He also dinched out the cigarette in the raw earth.

Carrying his suitcase, he returned the pillow to the office. "Morning."

The proprietor was up and having himself some bacon and eggs at a little table. "Have a good sleep?"

"You bet."

"Sit down and have a bite with me."

"I was thinking of maybe skipping breakfast."

"And cheat your body, eh? C'mon, sit down. I'll throw this breakfast in with the rest for the dollar."

"Well now, I appreciate that."

"I know you do. Bite in."

Fred sat across from the tall proprietor. He helped himself to bacon and eggs and a slice of toast. He

119

finished with a cup of coffee.

"Well, how was that, son?"

"Hit the spot, sir."

"Good. Now go out and tackle the world."

Fred smiled. "It's good to run into a man who's cheerful in the morning."

"If your tail ain't up in the morning, it sure as heck ain't gonna be up at night."

Fred decided the man meant that as a pun. He laughed. He got up and picked up his suitcase. "Thanks for everything."

"Drop by again. And the next time, let's hope you're rich."

Fred strolled down to Highway 16.

Fred hadn't more than set down his suitcase, and was about to unlimber his thumb, when who should be coming down the pike some distance off but Miss Minerva Baxter in her Super Six Essex.

Actually Fred wasn't too surprised. She'd pulled that stunt before. But if she wasn't stopping in the Black Hills, where in God's name was she stopping? Maybe she was going all the way around the world.

Then Miss Minerva spotted him. Her brown eyes were just high enough to clear the steering wheel. She stared; almost forgot she was driving; began heading for the shoulder of the road he was standing on; then, with a jerk, recovered and got back into her lane. As she rolled toward him at about ten miles an hour, it could be seen she was thinking a mile a minute. It was obvious she hadn't expected to see him hitchhiking again, but now that she had, she was busy reconsidering if she shouldn't pick him up once more. At the same time she was also remembering what she'd told him.

Fred gave her the slow thumb.

Miss Minerva rolled on about a block; then made up

her mind. Her head fastened on the list of driving instructions stuck on her windshield and she began shifting down, from high to second, from second to low, with the car at last choking to a stop. She stopped dead in her lane, right in the way of traffic. Luckily there were no cars behind her.

Fred grabbed up his suitcase and ran after her. He approached her on the driver's side. "Hi."

"Yes."

"Want me to drive again?"

"Would you please?" She was embarrassed, a little, and slid out from under the steering wheel and settled over on the passenger side.

Fred threw his suitcase in the back on top of her belongings and slipped under the wheel. He glanced up at the rear view mirror. Still no cars coming down on their tail. Quickly he started the motor and shifted smoothly into gear and they were on their way.

The first mile neither one said anything. Groves of ponderosa pine slid by.

Finally Fred smiled a Doon, Iowa smile. "Well, I see your brother's moved on. Farther west."

Her head sank a little.

Fred didn't have the heart to stick it into her any further. "You were right though. You didn't know me from Adam and in your situation you'd be a fool to trust a stranger."

She still said nothing.

Fred drove another mile. "Miss Minerva, this is going to be our second day together, and we're in the way of becoming old friends, so don't you think you can at least tell me where your brother really lives?"

"Boise."

"Idaho?"

"Yes. He has a ranch there."

121

"Hey. That far." Boise was on the other side of Wyoming, beyond Yellowstone National Park. If he behaved himself he had a ride practically all the way to his friend Don in Belgrade, Montana.

The gravel road become rough, irregular patches of washboard, occasional deep ruts. A sign read: "You are now leaving South Dakota and entering Wyoming." The country was all one, long rolling hills black with pine to the south and open country bumpy with eroding red soil to the north.

The town of Beulah had only a few buildings: a half-dozen houses, several stores, a filling station, a corral. It lay nestled above a heavily wooded stream. The stream had cut itself sharp red banks.

Miss Minerva continued to sit quietly beside him. She hadn't liked changing her mind.

Fred examined her with more care. Earlier he'd guessed her to be in her forties, but a second look at the skin over the backs of her hands and around her eyes told him she was perhaps around thirty-five. He noticed that the ink stains on her fingers had faded some. She'd probably scrubbed her hands with soap and water the night before. Her hair had a good healthy brown color. Her face was round and well-shaped. She'd probably been very pretty when she was twenty. Except for that sourpuss grimace on her lips she could still be considered goodlooking. She still had on that brown pleated skirt and tan blouse and both had begun to show the mold of her sturdy body. She was built a lot like Cousin Alice. He'd once dreamed of spooning with Alice, but poor timing and hovering relatives had prevented that.

He wondered if there wasn't some way he could get stern Miss Minerva to laugh. He bet that if he could get her to smile once her lips would become pink peony petals again.

122

There had to be a tragedy in her life somewhere. Some guy had probably promised to marry her and then had backed off. She'd given herself to the fellow and hadn't liked it. When he didn't call her again, she'd come to hate the memory of that one night of love.

Too bad she was thirty-five. If she'd been twenty-five, or even twenty-nine, he might have made a pitch for her. The three or seven years difference between his age and hers wouldn't have been too much of a stumbling block. He was in control around her. With Special Face he had been timorous, afraid of what to do next. But with this woman, had he been so inclined, he could have moved in on her like a masterful stallion. He was her superior. The boss. He even detected in himself a little streak of cruelty. Too bad. They could have had a great time spooning together across the state of Wyoming.

The highway wound through rolling woodlands and across deep red gulches. Surprisingly the rising hills were covered with bright pink roses. The perfume of them entered the car window and mingled pleasantly with the sweet smell of the hot engine.

The highway took a turn left and became a smooth tar road again. The rattling in the car vanished. Ahead and below a lovely broad valley opened before them. There were droves of cattle everywhere in the bottoms. The grass was an even green. Straight ahead lay the little village of Sundance and beyond it on the left towered Sundance Mountain.

Sundance was mostly a county courthouse, several stores, two saddleshops, two filling stations, and a couple dozen houses set anywhichway on a hillside. Four old Fords stood gleaming in the early morning sun. Two saddled ponies, heads lowered, tails flourishing, waited outside a harness shop.

123

For no reason at all Fred suddenly remembered a funny scene from home.

. . . . Aunt Kathryn and Uncle Clarence were over visiting one summer day. All the kids, Fred, Ed, Floyd, and the rest were outdoors playing football. Fred had found the football in the town dump. It had two holes in its rubber bladder and he'd patched them up with Pa's tire patching, and though the bladder still leaked a little it usually stayed hard long enough for the kids to play with an hour or so. Pa and Ma, and Aunt Kathryn and Uncle Clarence, watched the kids play. They smiled at all the antics of the kids as they booted the ball back and forth. Floyd, who was five years younger than Fred, was the best kicker.

Finally Pa couldn't resist joining the game. He had to show them how far he could kick the ball. The kids all backed up to receive the ball. They laughed ahead of time, already appreciating what a great kick Pa was going to make. Pa made a great face . . . swung his long leg into it and completely missed the ball. The kids thought that rather strange. Pa never had any trouble catching them in the butt with his toe when he set out to punish them for one thing or another.

Floyd finally ran up to show Pa how to hold the ball. Pa tried twice more, and only managed to fub the ball each time.

And then Aunt Kathryn decided to speak up. "Shucks," she said, "it should be easy to kick that thing. Give it here." To the great astonishment of Uncle Clarence her husband, and even more Pa and Ma, Aunt Kathryn picked up her long skirts and tucked them into her leather belt, revealing long thin calves and stringy thighs all the way to her tight black bloomers, and took the ball and held it in front of her as though

about to present the President with a gift, then took several skipping steps and let fly with her pointy right toe. Holy cow. She kicked her leg so high above her head that for a second she resembled a scissors opened too far. Pung! And the ball sailed completely over the corncrib.

There was a moment of utter amazement. Everybody's mouth hung open.

Pa was the first to break free. His lips began to talk without sound. Then he burst out laughing, and laughed so hard he finally had to bend over at the waist. The others followed. The yard rang with their laughter.

But Aunt Kathryn coolly unhooked her long skirts from her belt and shook them down over her pointy shoes. She said, "You people have all let yourself get too stiff in the hips. You want to keep yourself limber at all times" . . . .

Fred had to laugh outloud about it again. That Aunt Kathryn, who was so strict when it came to proper manners, could be so loose in the hips . . . man alive.

Miss Minerva asked, "What's so funny?"

"Nothing. Just something I happened to remember about my Aunt Kathryn."

Miss Minerva took offense. "You mean, you're really laughing at me and my old-fashioned ways."

"No, really. It had nothing to do with you."

Miss Minerva leveled her brown eyes at Fred. "I know I'm comical to you modern kids. But I can't help it. I am who I am and I have a right to be who I am."

"Of course, Miss Minerva. I meant no harm. Really."

The road headed northwest into a cluster of hills. Yellow grass lay over them like smooth folds of silk.

Fred pointed. "Isn't that beautiful land. I don't like to

126

use the word beautiful, but it really fits here. Wonderful for cattle. Make a perfect setting for a great cowboy novel."

Miss Minerva was still angry. "I have a right to be who I am. And don't you forget it either."

Fred fell silent.

The road followed a narrow cut through some hills studded with tree stumps. A dead animal lay on the road, circled by magpies. As the old Essex approached, the magpies flew up, scolding angrily, tails snapping.

"What was that?" Miss Minerva asked.

"Looked like a bobcat."

"Ugh."

The road opened on a different valley. It had a lifeless look about it: abandoned ranch buildings, fallen corrals, and collapsed log cabins. There was little grass along the banks of a dry coulee.

Again the road curved up a long slope of a hill. As they crested it, a gray shaft of rock appeared on a farther range of hills. Even from the top of their hill it had an immense look about it.

"By gummy," Fred exclaimed, "that must be the Devil's Tower I've been reading about. Look at it."

Miss Minerva looked unwillingly.

A junction sign came up, pointing north: *Devil's Tower, 7 miles.*

Fred slowed down. "How about it, have we got time for a quick look?"

"Must we?"

"Well, it's your car. Though I know if it was my car I'd sure go for a look. That's what I went west for. To see the sights."

Miss Minerva sighed. "Oh, all right. If it makes you happy. You are doing the driving for me and deserve something for that."

127

"Great." Fred turned the wheel over and headed up a gravel road. The road dipped several times, but the gray monolith remained in view all the way. At first it began to stick out of the surrounding country like a great petrified tree stump. But as they got to within a mile of it the tower began to look like something else. It made Fred wonder why in all those stories about Paul Bunyan, the mighty tree faller, someone hadn't called it Paul's Pecker. Because that's what it looked like. An enormous erection.

The last mile the tower of gray rock really began to rise over them. Fred guessed it was at least a quarter of a mile high. Its gray rock edge was precise and sharp against the north blue sky. It made the eye blink it was so vividly outlined.

"Look at that thing. My God in heaven."

"Please. No swearing."

"Wonder what caused it."

Fred pulled up in front of a low dark-brown building. The sign over the door read: *Devil's Tower Monument Museum.* Fred got out and stepped around behind the car and stared up at the great erect thing.

After he'd looked up at the tower a while, he noticed that Miss Minerva was still sitting in the car. "Aren't you at least going to get out to stretch your legs?"

"I guess I will at that." But after she got out, Miss Minerva turned her back on the tower and took the path down to the ladies privy instead.

"For goshsakes, that's almost an insult," Fred muttered.

Fred scrambled up a path leading through collapsed tallus and occasional fallen pine, on up to the top of a rocky ridge. The great gray shaft rose out of the ridge like a sword being brandished out of a massive hand.

He stopped to lean back on his heels, mouth open, to

128

look up to its top. Bone inside his head cracked a little.

The shaft appeared to be made of many five-sided molten columns, all of them fluted, and narrowing as they flowed into the summit. Near the top the symmetry of the columns were marred by erosion and broken sections. The sides of the tower were utterly stark, with not a bit of growth to be seen, neither grass nor bush nor tree. Only at the top, where it flattened off, could tufts of grass be made out.

It made a man feel great to look at it.

Fred wondered what Special Face would think about it. He remembered she'd once gone to New York and had written to a friend back home that she thought the Empire State Building "thrilling." At the time, because he'd already begun to collect words in his little leather word-book, he'd wondered if she knew the old meaning of the word "thrill."

Fred read several lines of lettering on a large wooden sign. He learned that the outcropping of sedimentary rocks on which the Tower stood was six hundred feet above the Belle Fourche River and that the Tower itself was six hundred feet high. Some 20,000,000 years ago the land in the general Black Hills area had been boosted upward and in that particular spot upwelling lava had punched through the surface of the earth and formed a blister. It was during the lava's rapid cooling that massive molten columns were formed in the shape of prisms.

Fred walked halfway around the tower, picking his way over dead branches in the standing pine. The tower wasn't perfectly round. It was shaped more like a twin rhubarb stalk blunted at the top. After a while, listening to the sounds around, Fred thought he could hear the great thing humming. The hum of it was like a metronome about to vibrate.

Fred looked down the slope through the pines. Sure enough, Miss Minerva was back in her car, looking down at her hands. What an unimaginative creature. It was high time somebody gave her the royal goose. Put the prod to her. Lord.

Fred had a call to nature himself. He looked around to see if the ranger below could see him. The ranger couldn't. No other sightseers were around either. Fred relieved himself at the foot of Devil's Tower.

Fred got back into the old Essex both sobered as well as exhilarated by what he'd just seen. It was like he'd first been flattened and then stretched by the majestic pillar of columnar prisms. Miss Minerva, however, sat unmoved, patient, waiting like before.

Shrugging, Fred turned the key, touched the starter, backed up the car, and headed for Highway 16 again.

The rest of the forenoon neither one had much to say. The little towns of Moorcroft and Gillette and Wild Cat went by. Highway 16 continued to be smooth black tar. Spotted Horse was only a post office with a store and a filling station. Beyond Powder River they came upon bands of sheep nibbling at thin forage over barren brown hills. On the other side of Ucross they tooled past handsome brick ranch houses.

As they approached Buffalo, Wyoming, a rising dark bulk once again shouldered up out of the landscape ahead. It sharpened very rapidly into various peaks. Several of them were snow-capped.

Fred leaned ahead for a better look. "That's got to be the Big Horn Mountains. Now we'll see the real Shining Mountains at last."

Miss Minerva wasn't in the least interested in watching the land ahead erupt once more into massive formations of rock. She looked at the gas gauge. "Quarter full. We better stop up ahead there in Buffalo."

130

"Good idea."

Miss Minerva managed a little smile. "You've driven very well, Mister Feikema. And for that I think you deserve a lunch of some kind."

"I can pay for my own food."

"No, you've driven very well and I'm most appreciative."

They eased into Buffalo. Fred liked the ranch town immediately. Through the open car window came the fresh smell of mountain air. Main street looked like it had been laid down along a winding cow trail. Most frame buildings had false fronts. Some of the stone buildings had fronts done in an original frontier style. West of town low slopes blended off into folded foothills. The foothills in turn shelved up into steep mountain ridges.

Miss Minerva pointed. "Let's stop at that Standard station ahead there. I see a hamburger stand across the street from it."

Fred pulled up beside the nearest gas pump. He got out slowly, knees stiff from sitting so long in a tight car. He stretched himself, rising on his toes, taking in a great breath of the high clean air.

Miss Minerva got out slowly too. She took the car keys with her. She told the station attendant to fill the car with gas. "And be sure to check the oil and water."

"Yes, mam."

Fred had noted the last while that the car seemed to ride like a box wagon. "Yes, and while you're at it, check the tires too, will you? They felt hard to me."

The attendant, a bowlegged fellow wearing cowboy boots, nodded. "Tires pick up air in hot weather."

Miss Minerva extracted a single dollar bill from her purse. "Mister Feikema, would you go across the street and get us each a hamburger and a bottle of pop?"

131

Fred took the green bill. "You wouldn't want to go in and sit at a table?"

"I think I'll eat my lunch walking around a little. Get my blood to circulating."

"Okay. What kind of pop?"

"Cream soda."

"Ah. My favorite too."

Fred went across the street and called in his order through a little window.

Several sun-wizened cowboys strolled by, boots clicking on the concrete sidewalks. They'd just ridden into town and had tied their saddle horses to a telephone pole. Farther down on a low bridge over a creek a dozen men stood talking. One of the men, a very white old-timer, was holding a fishing pole. Further on the creek curved through an expanse of thick pasture grass right in the middle of town. The scent of the fresh grass amongst the buildings was especially sweet.

"Here's your burgers and cream soda."

"Thanks." Fred placed the dollar bill on the counter and got back seventy cents in change.

Miss Minerva was waiting for him, a hungry look in her eye. She set her pop on the hood of the car and then carefully unfolded the wax paper from the hamburger. She took a deep sniff of the meat between the bread, then looked at Fred with an apologetic smile. "Just making sure the meat wasn't spoiled."

Fred smiled back. "Around here you don't have to worry. They're all fresh meat people."

Miss Minerva nodded. She took a good healthy bite, followed it with a good sip of cream soda.

It was the first time Fred had seen Miss Minerva do something hearty.

After they finished eating, Fred brought the two empty bottles back to the hamburger stand, and Miss

132

Minerva settled her bill with the station attendant.

"Thanks for the grub, Miss Minerva," Fred said.

"You deserved it."

"Well, I guess it's time to head out again, eh?" Fred started for the driver's side.

"Just a moment." Miss Minerva touched him on the elbow. "I was just thinking."

Fred let her hand rest on him for a second, and then, with fine delicacy, withdrew his elbow. "Yes?"

"I was just thinking now would be a good time for me to learn how to drive in the mountains. I have a good driver with me to teach me how."

Fred thought: "Oh, Lord. Now watch my stomach get tighter than a freighter's knot."

Miss Minerva gave Fred a great smile. "Don't you think?"

Fred hitched himself up, first on one side, then the other. "Well, it's your car."

"Good." Miss Minerva extracted the car key from her purse and got in. She settled herself solidly behind the wheel, all business.

Fred got in on the other side, very reluctantly. He considered leaving her. But the thought of what might happen to her driving alone in the mountains made him feel guilty about deserting her. He could just see her rolling off some high mountain pass somewhere.

Miss Minerva started the motor. "You enjoy the scenery so much you should give your full attention to it. Except for those moments when you're telling me what not to do."

Fred cast her a sidelong glance. The lady was capable of sarcasm.

Following the typed instructions on the windshield, pedaling and shifting gears, Miss Minerva soon had them rolling. She got the car up to thirty miles an hour

133

and then held to it. They cruised out into open ranch country. The tar road changed to ruggly gravel.

For a dozen miles on level land Miss Minerva didn't do too badly. She'd picked up a few of Fred's driving mannerisms by just watching. She no longer kept working the wheel back and forth as she drove but held it steady. She drove with her hands positioned on the bottom of the steering wheel instead of at the top. Fred had to admire her. She might not have a wild hair, but she at least dared to take a chance.

They followed Clear Creek up a winding canyon and then climbed up through heavily wooded slopes. The old Super Six Essex had the power, and Miss Minerva didn't have to shift down.

Miss Minerva allowed herself a quiet smile of satisfaction. "Just you watch the sights now, you hear?"
Fred nodded.

They mounted a wide sweeping plateau. Long slopes of beautiful standing pine, broken by occasional meadows of the greenest grass, opened ahead of them in a vast V. The V slowly but imperceptibly lifted up into dark hilltops. There were lovely trickling streams of very clear water everywhere. Cattle grazed in scattered groups as far as the eye could see.

"South Dakota could sure use some of this."

"What?" Miss Minerva kept her eye on the speedometer to make sure she had the right speed for the gear she was in.

Muddy Ranger Station came into view on their right. Two green pickups stood outside.

Fred said, "Maybe we should stop and ask how the road is up above." Fred was secretly hoping that after they got out he could somehow maneuver himself behind the wheel again.

"We're going all right, aren't we?"

"I guess so."

Mountain jays flew up off the road ahead. They'd been feeding on some horse droppings. "Clack-ak! clack-ak!" they squalled, black crests stiffly erect. Fred noted that their markings were different from the jays he'd known on the prairies. The mountain jay blue was an intense cobalt.

"Aren't we doing all right?"

"Sure. Steady as you go." Fred had the feeling that his whole left side, cheek, shoulder, thigh, had become a separate being with an extra set of eyes concentrated on her driving. "You're doing fine."

The road made a turn left and began to climb. Soon their ears began to crack.

Around a second turn, to the right, they came upon road graders at work. The Wyoming Highway Department was widening the road. The gravel became loose red dirt.

Miss Minerva, eyes on the speedometer, noted they'd fallen below twenty-five miles an hour, and immediately shifted down to second. The road graders saw the car coming and got out of the way. The begrimed men watched them go by with a shake of the head. The smell of raw red mountain earth was like the sweet fresh manure of colts. Two miles farther on the new grading ended and they once again rattled along on ribbed gravel. Miss Minerva shifted back to high. Muddy Creek tumbled rough and brownish alongside the road.

On the next bend in the road the climb stiffened very sharply. Before Miss Minerva could shift down the car began to miss and to chug. But the moment she got the car into second it took hold even and powerful again. A quarter of a mile later the climb became even steeper and again the motor began to miss and to chug. Miss Minerva shifted down into low.

135

Fred tried not to watch her driving. At the same time he was absolutely sure that in a couple of minutes things were going to get wild. He tried to concentrate on the landscape, noting that the timber had opened up and become sparse, that the grass was once more pale and dry like it was back on the dry plains. Many little springs trickled out of the roadside cut, some of them piling up behind self-made dirt dams and spilling palely across the gravel road.

"I think I'd speed up a little," Fred said.

Miss Minerva glanced at the card of instructions on the windshield. "But I'm almost doing fifteen miles an hour."

"Well?"

"But if I go over fifteen I'll have to shift up into second and then she'll start to chug on us again."

"It won't hurt to go over fifteen miles an hour in low. Then you'll have more power in low. And you may need it up ahead."

"But the instructions say —"

"— the heck with the instructions. Just listen to me. I know."

"But —"

"— didn't you just say back in Buffalo that you were glad to have me with you because I was a good driver who could teach you?"

"Yes, I think I did."

"Well then, speed up a little or the first thing you know the motor'll miss even in low. The air up here is very thin."

But Miss Minerva didn't speed up. Her chin came down grimly and her brown eyes turned stubborn.

With an effort Fred turned his head away and again tried to look at the scenery. The scape became even more barren. Enormous jagged granite peaks shoved up

136

around them. Fred thought it hostile cold-hearted country. Yet it was also very beautiful. In some of the steep high north valleys lay great drifts of old yellow snow. There were tiny dots of color everywhere, white, blue, yellow, even orange, and when Fred looked more closely he saw that the varied dots were tiny flowers growing in moss-covered tundra.

His ears cracked. He swallowed to clear them. The smell of old snow reminded him of a frozen piece of chocolate cake he'd once eaten in grade school.

The highway veered around to the right; became extremely steep. Off on their left a sheer dropoff thousands of feet deep wheeled into view. The sensation was as if the continent were dropping away from them and they were left on the only remaining high ground.

The old Essex began to cough. As Fred had feared it was having trouble firing in the rarefied air.

"Give her some gas!" Fred cried. "Step down on that footfeed."

"Nevermind now. I'm doing the driving."

"That's just the trouble. Step on the gas, woman!"

Miss Minerva stubbornly refused to step on it.

Fred's belly became as tight as a snare drum.

The view beyond the left front fender of the Essex became sensational. Vaguely, far down, a little town could be made out in the light blue mist of a great distance. The blue atmosphere shaded off into varied tossing landscapes of brown and red and orange. The blue atmosphere made the colors work in lovely harmony. In the midst of it all a single bald eagle hung on air perfectly poised, unmoving, as if stuck into the atmosphere with a taxidermist pin.

Fred could see they were near the top of the climb. Several hundred more yards and they'd make it. Ahead, on the right, was a large signboard. Squinting, Fred made out the legend:

MUDDY PASS
Elevation 9666 feet

The Super Six engine coughed again; choked; coughed; quit. The car chugged to a stop.

"Oh dear."

Fred's brain began to prickle like a limb having fallen asleep.

Miss Minerva studied the typed instructions on the windshield, began following them to the letter. She first put the gear in neutral. Then she touched the starter. The starter whirred; whirred. Nothing. There was only the desperately sucking sound of the carburetor.

The car began to roll backward.

Fred glanced over his shoulder. Because of the curve in the road he could see that if the car rolled a couple of dozen feet straight back it would sail off into space, falling God only knew how far. Something had to be done.

Fred lunged across in front of Miss Minerva, his left elbow catching her in the belly, and jerked back the handbrake by the door, while with his right hand he grabbed the steering wheel and turned it to make the rear wheels stay on the road.

Miss Minerva gasped. He'd hit her so hard in the belly he'd knocked her breath out. "Uh . . .uh . . ."

Next with his left hand he shoved the shift into high gear. The gears under the floorboard crashed.

"The-uh . . . nerve-uh . . ."

Both the handbrake and the dead engine began to take hold. Chug . . . chugg . . . chuggg . . .

Again Fred glanced over his shoulder. The car was rolling dangerously close to the loose gravel along the edge of the road. Beyond the edge he caught a glimpse

138

of a depth he had trouble believing. The dropoff at that point was tremendous. It had to be a precipice of at least a thousand feet. God.

Chug-ugg. And the car stopped dead.

"Get out!" Fred commanded.

Miss Minerva got her breath back. "Uch." Instantly she flew at him like some old brood hen robbed of her eggs. "Why, you terrible man, hitting me in the stomach like that! Why, I have half a mind —"

"Get out of the car!"

"— to ask you to get out of the car and make you walk the rest of the . . . what?"

"Get out of the car so I can slide over under the wheel. Because I'm driving from here on in."

"Swearing at me?"

"Woman, you damned near killed us with your damnable dilatory reading of those silly instructions."

"Dilatory? What's that mean? Why, you —"

"Will you get out from under that wheel? Because so help me God if you don't, I'll jump out and let you roll off the mountain by yourself."

"— ruffian you!"

"Take a look for yourself back there then."

With an outraged look she slowly twisted around in the seat and looked back. "Oh!"

"Yes!"

"Oh dear."

"Yes. And now will you please for sweet Jesus' sake get out from under that wheel? There'll be just enough room for you to walk around in front of the car and get in on my side here."

"Oh dear."

When she still didn't move, but sat there exclaiming mildly, Fred gave her another punch in the belly with his left elbow, lighter though than before, and then gave

139

her thigh a good pinch.

The pinch did it. "Oh dear," and she got out deftly.

"Just hang onto the side of the car and you'll be all right."

"Yes yes."

The moment she was out Fred carefully slid over under the wheel and got control of the old car. He waited until she'd got in on the passenger side. Then, half-twisting in the seat and looking back, he carefully let out the brake a little and then pushed in the clutch a bit and let the Essex start rolling again. He let it roll until the right rear bumper caught on a projecting rock in the cut on the right side of the road. Then, safe, Fred let out a great breath. "Wow."

The two of them sat very still for a moment. There was only the loud cracking of the sinuses inside the head.

Fred said, "I'm going to set that a carburetor a little richer so we can get out of here. The next thing you know another wild-eyed tourist will be on our tail." He got out and opened the hood to see what tools he needed. "Do you have a screwdriver in the car?"

"Yes." Miss Minerva moved in jerks. "In here." She pawed through the glove compartment and came up with a brown-handled screwdriver.

Fred reset the screw on the choke. Then he closed the hood and got in behind the wheel. He handed back the screwdriver. "Now." He turned the key and pushed the starter. The starter whirred several times, and then, miracles of miracles, the engine fired. It coughed a few times; then leveled into an even purr. Presently it ran merrily. "Good."

In a moment he had the car in gear and they proceeded to the top of the pass.

"May our merciful God be thanked," Miss Minerva

whispered.

The road down the other side of the mountain was even steeper. At times the hairpin turns were so tight Fred had to put her in low, with the brakes on, and wheel her hard left and hard right, elbows swinging back and forth. There were great gaping canyons off the edge of the road, first on the left, then on the right. The turns were so tight it sometimes looked as though the road were going straight off into space.

Miss Minerva had to look and yet hated to look. She couldn't believe she was where she was. When the dropoffs became even more pronounced, she finally couldn't take it any longer and leaned forward, hiding her face in her hands on her knees.

Fred was still angry. About halfway down they came to a curve he was sure was meant to shoot them off into space. There was no way the highway engineers could have completed the curve around the sheer rock on the left.

Miss Minerva asked, voice muffled, "Is the road getting any better?"

Fred smiled. She'd given him such a scare she deserved one good jolt in turn. "Yep. In a minute we'll be in heaven."

Very gradually she raised her head. When her eyes came up level with the bottom of the windshield and she saw what there was to see, that the road speared off into nothing, space, she gulped; dropped her face down on her knees. "Mercy sakes!"

Fred laughed. At the same time it surprised him that he sometimes could be mean to people.

"You fooled me!" she cried muffled into her knees.

In the late afternoon sun the rock walls of the canyon had a smooth satiny red color. It struck Fred that here would have been the perfect place to stick Devil's

141

Tower.

Fred let the motor drag as much as he could, braked hard, gritted his teeth, wheeled her over a hard careful left. And made the deadly curve.

Fred drove carefully around two more curves.

And then the road leveled and at last straightened out. All around them towered great granite rocks. The shadows off the staggered mountains enveloped them in deep purple dusk.

Fred turned on the lights.

Miss Minerva heard the click. "Is it all right now?"

Fred let down. "Yes, Miss Minerva. You can look up now. We've finally made it to the bottom."

Again she raised her head, cautiously. When she saw that, yes, truly the canyons were gone and the land was leveling off, she let go with a vast sigh. "Merciful Father in heaven." She took a deep breath, and then said, softly, "That was a dirty trick, Frederick." It was the first time she'd called him by his given name.

"I know."

"It was very mean of you."

"Yes. And I apologize."

She sniffled back a few tears.

Fred said, "And I must admit I also should have had my wits about me in the first place. I should have had that carburetor set richer back there in Buffalo. I just wasn't thinking, I guess."

The lights of Tensleep swung into view around a curve. A filling station, a grain elevator, several stores and saddleshops lined both sides of a wide graveled street, all of them false-front frame buildings. A dance pavilion stood set back on a lot by itself. Across the street from the pavilion stretched a row of gray tourist cabins. A bright light burned over the door of a nearby cafe.

Miss Minerva cleared her throat. "I think we should

142

stop here. We've had enough for today."

"Okay by me."

"We'll get us a cabin first and freshen up, and then go have us a bite to eat."

"I can sleep outdoors under the pines."

"No. You drove wonderfully through those wretched mountains. I insist on paying for a cabin for you."

"Well, if you say so." Fred felt he had earned a good night's rest at that.

"Drive over to the office there."

Fred pulled up in front of the far cabin and shut off the engine.

"Thank goodness we arrived safe." She got out and brushed down her dress. "I'll be back in a moment." She vanished into the office.

Fred got out too, and rolled his shoulders. The muscles over his back were still tight. "I don't want to go through that again. What a dame."

Presently Miss Minerva came back dangling two keys. "We have the two end cabins there. Would you drive the car down in front of the No. 11 cabin please?"

Fred got into the old Essex again and parked it in front of Cabin No. 11.

Miss Minerva gave him the key for Cabin No. 12. "Why don't you freshen up a little and then we'll eat." She offered him what was meant to be a sweet smile, buttering him up a little. "All right?"

Fred got out his suitcase and made himself at home in No. 12. A sharp smell of insecticide hung in the air. The bed was neatly made covered by a thick brown horse blanket. The floor was covered by yellow linoleum, matching the top of the little table and the border around the sink. There was a big window in front and a small window in back. Fred washed up. Gradually his neck muscles relaxed.

Miss Minerva called him. "Are you ready, Frederick? I'm famished."

"Coming." Fred wasn't sure he liked being called Frederick by Miss Minerva. Only Special Face had that right. It was what his mother used to call him.

They strolled across the thick grass toward the cafe. Miss Minerva chattered like a magpie about that awful ride through the mountains. "It's an outrage really that the highway department of the State of Wyoming doesn't give a stranger some kind of warning ahead of time what that road will be like through the mountains. With no guard rails, and very poor signs indicating sharp turns, it's a wonder people aren't dashed to their deaths in droves. Really. When I get home I shall write them a letter about it. To the Governor. Yes, I shall."

Fred noticed that a sharp spotlight had come on across the street in front of the dance pavilion. Several cars were already parked out in front of it and a dozen saddle horses were hitched to a rail. Big doings were on for the night.

"Not everybody can drive a car like you and make it over the top safely. Most people are very poor drivers. Imagine what would happen if all the poor drivers in America were to decide to take a vacation at the same time and drive through the Big Horns . . . why, like I say, those canyons would be piled full of wrecked cars and dead bodies. Och! when I think of what almost happened to us today, why, it's a wonder I didn't have palpitations of the heart."

Single horsemen, and teams hitched to rigs, and old battered pickups began to arrive from all directions and pull up in front of the pavilion. Single horsemen, like any driver of a car, had to hold out their hand too to show which way they meant to turn.

"They're going to hear about this. We tourists just

144

simply can't tolerate such wretched driving conditions. That was a U.S. Highway, wasn't it?"

"Yes, Miss Minerva." Fred held the door open for her and they entered the cafe. "Good old U.S. Highway 16."

"Well, then they shall surely hear from me. And while I'm at it, I think I shall also write the President." Miss Minerva, clasping her purse tightly to her bosom, looked up and down two rows of booths. After a bite on her nether lip, she choose the end booth.

There were a couple dozen other customers, cowboys, several tourist couples, and a collection of young people.

A slender girl waiter, not more than fourteen, brought them each a menu. The menus were old, much-fingered, stained with varied ovals of grease.

Miss Minerva took both menus and began reading the listings. "I'm going to order you the largest T-bone steak they have. As well as a good-sized one for myself. We deserve it."

Fred wasn't sure he liked that. Miss Minerva was beginning to act possessive. It'd once been all right that Ma'd been possessive. Ma'd loved him in a noble manner. And it would have been all right if Special Face had been possessive. God, if only Special Face had been possessive! That would have been the one way for him to have broken out of his tight caul of being shy around girls.

"What do you say to a large T-bone, Frederick?"

"I think that'd be wonderful."

The willowy young waitress wrote down the order in a jerky manner, with her fingers all squatted down. Fred noticed she had a quiet grey eye for him. The blue of her smock deepened the even grey in her eyes. Her hair was piled on top of her head in a large golden knot. Her

145

bosom had just begun to show above her wide leather belt. "Thank you," she said and hurried off with their orders.

Miss Minerva continued to rattle on and on. That incident up on Muddy Pass had really set her off.

A country band began to play in the pavilion across the street. The music came clear and loud through the open cafe windows.

Miss Minerva paused in mid-sentence. "My goodness, on top of everything else, that too?"

Fred lifted an eyebrow. "What's wrong with that?"

"Such music is of the devil!"

"Maybe after dinner we can go over and have ourselves a good fling before we take on the next mountain pass," he teased.

"Never. Bodies close like that. Nothing good can come from it."

Fred had heard that argument all his life from Calvinist ministers. He himself thought dancing wonderful and liked to brag that Pa in his youth had been a expert square dance caller and fiddler.

The pretty solemn-eyed maiden soon came with their T-bone steaks. The steaks were served smoking hot in iron frying pans, with side dishes set out in another tray.

Miss Minerva's eyes opened in astonishment. "My, they're liberal with food in this country."

"That's the West for you."

Miss Minerva sprinkled on some salt and pepper, and some sauce to bring up the taste just right for her tongue, and then once again acted hearty. She picked up her steak knife and went after her meat with gleaming teeth. She chewed. "My, this is good. Ohh." Juice ran at the corners of her lips and she dabbed at it with her paper napkin. "Isn't this delicious?"

Fred nodded, busy cutting and eating himself. He

146

didn't like to put on much condiment, preferring the natural taste of the meat. Out of the corner of his eye he noted that Miss Minerva's lips seemed to have thickened. She had it in her all right to be an eager lover.

Between bites Miss Minerva sipped at her tea. It was curious to see the difference between the way she tackled her meat and the way she sipped her tea. The one she wolfed down and the other she savored daintly.

The beat of the music became louder. Fred found himself tapping his toe to the rhythm of it. Once his high knee touched the table, jiggling the water in their glasses.

Miss Minerva paused in the middle of a bite. She looked exactly like a heavy-jawed cat with a mouse in its mouth. "You are drawn to the enticements of Satan, aren't you?"

"You mean, the enticements of the Lord, don't you?"

It was about the worst thing he could have said. Her face turned severe, hard, "I suppose after we're through eating here you'll go over to that den of iniquity."

"I'm thinking about it."

"And I suppose afterwards you'll walk some tramp girl home?"

Fred laughed. "That popular with girls I'm not. I'm too much of a freak for that."

"I noticed that girl waitress looking at you."

"Oh, she's probably just got a wild hair for boys."

"I see your mother never scrubbed your tongue with soap."

Fred laughed again. "Funny thing is my mother once did make me wash out my mouth with soap."

"She really did?"

"Yeh. I once said our justice of peace back home liked little boys too much. When she scolded me, I

147

quoted her a text out of the Bible about sodomy."

Miss Minerva swelled up in outrage.

"I'm sorry."

"I'll bet you are." Miss Minerva finished chewing her meat; swallowed it. "You're going to that dance hall then after we eat?"

"Yeh, I think I will. Just to have a look around. I hardly doubt anybody will ask me to dance though."

She glared down at what was left of her steak. She nodded to herself; once. "We'll see about that."

They finished their meal in troubled silence.

Miss Minerva was the first to get up. She went over to the cashier and took some dollar bills out of her purse and ruffled them one by one to make sure two bills weren't stuck together and paid for them both. Then she led the way outside. It was with an effort she got control of herself. With a brief glance at the dance pavilion, she asked, "You'll at least be wanting to wash up first though, won't you? Change your shirt maybe?"

"Yeh, I guess I will at that."

She started them both for their cabins. When she got to her cabin she hesitated a moment before going in.

Fred went on to his cabin, got out his key, opened up and stepped inside, leaving the key in the door.

Fred was drying his face, when he heard a click in the door behind him. Whirling around, he knew right away what had happened. "I'll be damned." Miss Minerva had locked him in. "I always did have the bad habit of leaving the key in the door." He could just see the cat-got-the-canary look in her face.

Then he began to laugh right outloud. By golly. That old witch. "Well, at least thank God she ain't one of those older women who has a yen for young boys." He hung up his towel.

The little square window in back caught his eye. He

148

went over to check it. It was almost head high. He opened the window and inspected the screen. The screen was held in place with two small hooks. Aha. Here was the way he could get out. Provided of course he could squeeze his big shoulders through. He'd wait until it got dark and then make his escape.

He lay down on bed a while and relaxed. He kicked off his oxfords, letting them drop to the floor. He loosened his tie and let his chin ride down inside his shirt collar. He stretched. The music from the dance pavilion came to him faintly.

He smiled to himself when he remembered how up on Muddy Pass he'd punched Miss Minerva in the belly with his elbow. She'd had a firm flat belly. A boxer would have been proud of her hard gut. Then wondering what her breasts might be like, he napped.

He awoke with a start an hour later. In the dark he slipped over to the little square window and looked out. The light out front of the dance pavilion was shining very bright. The parking area was packed with jalopies and pickups and saddled horses. The music was louder than ever. Beyond the town the mountains loomed a dark black against the night sky.

He slipped on his oxfords in the dark, washed the cobwebs out of his eyes, and snugged up his tie. Then with a quiet smile, he studied the little square window again. If he went out head first, he'd have to land on his hands and there just might be a cactus or two growing in back of the cabin. So that was out. Best way was legs first. Very quietly he unhooked the screen and set it inside the cabin. Then he set a chair under the window, mounted it, turned and thrust first one leg through the little square opening and then the other. Slowly he wriggled his length through the opening. When he got to his shoulders, he reached his left arm through first, then angled out his left shoulder. Snug fit. His sweater caught on one of the eye-hooks and he had to work it loose. Next his right ear got caught. But cricking his chin deep into his collarbone, he scraped out, and at last with a little push dropped to the ground. He landed on grass, not cactus. He felt a little like a just-dropped calf. He stood stooped a moment, listening carefully, making sure Miss Minerva hadn't heard him hit the ground. Then, still smiling, he brushed himself off and headed for the dance pavilion.

When he entered he found the place lighted with old-time kerosene lanterns. There was a pause in the dancing. Couples and trios were busy laughing in groups all over the floor.

Presently a cowboy sitting on the floor in the far corner began to sing to himself without a guitar. The tune was The Dally Roper's Song and he was letting go with a lot of "cum a ti yipi yipi ayes" and some chuckles at himself at how funny it all sounded. His beard was bristly and his black hat was tossed back and his shirt collar was open four buttons down. With his swarthy face and dark hair he was very handsome but didn't seem to mind it. He fondled a dark bottle of whiskey. In a few moments he swung into Old Iron Pants Pete, still without a guitar. He sang eloquently: "He liked to mix mingle with mall."

The crowd stilled to listen to him. Some of the old timers began to smile. Now that was the real cowboy singing style.

Again the swarthy cowboy had several good laughs at how humorous he was. A pause, and then, tolling his curly dark head, hat almost tipping off, he rolled out The Hangman's Song:

> "Well, slack your rope, hangman,
> Slack it once more,

I see my true love ridin',
I see my true love once more."

Some of the young swains joined in on the refrain, voices uncertain, some a half-note too high, some a whole note too low. The cowboy shook his head at them to shut up, they were spoiling his act.

He next sang As I Went Walking One Morning For Pleasure. Again the cowboy allowed himself a few chuckles at his own expense as he went along. He'd had just enough to drink to enjoy getting attention:

"Well, if I must marry 'twill be to a widow
With a great big ranch and a ten-story home,
If I must marry 'twill be to a widow
With seventeen children not one of my own."

A hearty laugh spread through the pavilion. The dance band meanwhile began to reassemble up on the stand.

The cowboy had himself one last song, Streets of Loredo:

"As I walked out in the streets of Loredo,
As I walked out into old Loredo town,
I spied a poor cowboy all wrapped in white linen,
All wrapped in white linen
for they had gunned him down."

The cowboy's voice improved as he went along, and just before he hit the last line, his voice climbed an octave. That instant his voice suddenly purled over into a pure

152

lovely tenor, clear, right on the note, haunting.

Fred felt a catch in his throat.

Then the dance band swung into When The Work's All Done This Fall and couples began to square off and gyrate on the glistening floor.

Fred watched the couples glide by. Some young girls in long dresses giggled at his height. Fred found himself a chair.

He looked for a tall girl he might dance with. The whole shebang revolved past where he sat several times. He didn't see one, not even one moderately tall. Cowboy country apparently didn't breed tall girls.

For the fun of it he next looked for the prettiest girl on the floor. It took a while. When he did find her and had a good look at her on one of her turns, he was surprised to discover it was the willowly young waitress who'd served him at the cafe. Her fingers were squatted flat on her partner's back just like when she'd written up his order. Fred was further startled to see she wasn't a bit shy dancing. It made him a little sad to think she wasn't as innocent as he'd first thought.

The band swung into Turkey In The Straw and a dance caller began to intone the words. Everybody lined up at the corners. In a moment, with the tripping of women's heels and the stomping of men's boots, they were sashaying out the squares.

Again Fred watched the tossing heads for a tall girl. There weren't any.

Back home, before starting college, he'd gone to several square dances and had had trouble getting his feet organized. He had a good sense of time up in his head but not down in his toes.

He watched some of the boys helping themselves to snorts from a bottle. One coarse-featured woman of thirty, with a loud hoarse laugh, had a snort with them.

153

At last, having seen all there was to see, Fred got up and headed for the door. He was almost through the door when a slender hand caught him on the elbow. It was the willowy young waitress.

"What's the rush?" she asked. She gave him the same quiet grey eye she'd given him in the cafe. She liked him. Her piled up hair gleamed a bright gold.

"No rush. I just didn't see any tall girls for me."

"Shucks, what about me? I like my men tall."

It struck him she'd be easy. "But you're so young."

"Oh come on." She slid her arm warmly around his high waist. She hardly came to his chest. "I won't hurt you."

Fred shook his head. He was sure that, though only fourteen, she'd do it with him all right, but he wanted the first time to be with someone special. "You're awfully nice," he said, "but I'm too big for you. And too old. Thanks."

She looked at him a moment, then on an impulse, rising on her toes, she kissed him full on the lips. Then in a whip she was gone.

Fred slowly wiped her kiss off his lips.

He managed to crawl in through the little window again without Miss Minerva hearing him.

VII

The next morning Miss Minerva got up early and unlocked Fred's door and invited him to have breakfast with her. There was a marvelous scent of sage outdoors. Fred imagined he could still hear the echoes of last night's dance music under the murmuring cottonwoods along Tensleep Creek. Both Miss Minerva and Fred had pancakes and ham and coffee. Miss Minerva continued to be famished. The ink stains on her fingers had all but disappeared.

They gassed up, checked the oil, kicked rubber, and with Fred at the wheel were off down the curving gravel highway. They crossed the barren Nowood Creek, moving from the brilliant green of Tensleep's lawns into the red soil of an old badlands.

Neither had much to say. Miss Minerva was smiling to herself. She'd kept Fred from sin the night before. Fred was smiling to himself. He'd outwitted her.

There was no wind out and the sky was dazzling high. At that altitude the air was so thin one's lungs worked overtime. Fred found himself sitting very erect.

They crossed into an enormous mortar-shaped basin. The distant rims had the colors of blue Delft. Off to the east the flanks of the Big Horns were scarred by four great canyons. The previous dusk the old Essex had zigzagged down the canyon on the right. The whole range of the Big Horns stood stretched out in clear relief, with the shaggy bald head of Cloud Peak towering over it all.

Just before Worland the road become tar again. They cruised through a section of adobe houses. Darkskinned children played in raw orange dirt. Beyond the children lay beetfields. Fred guessed they were Mexican children, not Indian.

155

The town of Worland itself was handsome, lush green lawns, fine-looking gardens, fresh-painted houses. There was a sticky smell of sweetness about, and looking around Fred soon spotted the smokestacks of a sugar refinery on the southwest corner of town.

Then the road veered straight north. It followed the Big Horn River, up through Durkee, Rairden, and Manderson, all of them very small towns, with false front stores and corrals on the outskirts.

Basin drifted by. Fred liked its roomy four-block civic center, with a green commons, a library, a new post office, and a towering courthouse.

At Greybull the road turned west. Fred didn't care for Greybull. It stank of oil refineries. The little valley it sat in had the look of a raw red carcass scraped utterly clean of all fat.

The road lifted up on top of a long bench of land. It was a delight to find. It was irrigated with water from the Greybull River to the south and was covered with wonderful green square fields of alfalfa and beans and oats. In the very center of it rested the little village of Emblem. Fred thought it a perfect name for the place.

Fred didn't care much for Cody either. It had the cheap look of a town in the grip of tourist promoters. The streets were full of over-dressed guides and dude wranglers, bright silk shirts, whipcords, high-heeled polished boots, cowhide vests, and hats as big as dishpans. Only the buffed leather smelled good.

Miss Minerva didn't like the looks of Cody either. She sat glaring at all the noisy bustle. Her mouth fell back into that old set expression of hers as though she were about to scream at all the sin she was witnessing.

Outside Greybull they climbed up through sagecovered hills toward the Absaroka Range. Their ears began to crack and they had to swallow to clear

156

them. The road wriggled toward the mouth of the Shoshone Canyon. The entire roadway had been blasted out of an overhanging wall of sandstone and granite. In some places the road had been pinched into tight one-way tunnels where Fred had to turn on the headlights. Both he and Miss Minerva felt trapped in the dark tunnels. Another turn and they suddenly were looking up at the face of the Shoshone Dam.

Miss Minerva was shocked at the huge size of the dam. She grabbed Fred's arm. "Wait. Can't we take some other route?"

"Nope. I checked just before we started this morning. It's the only road through here."

"Suppose we meet another car coming along the edge of the dam there?"

"Well, it'll be more his neck than ours, since we'll be taking the inside lane against the wall." Fred shook off her hand. "Just sit tight. I'll get us through. After all, we did manage to negotiate the Big Horns."

Miss Minerva settled back in her seat.

Luckily the highway continued to be smooth tar. It resembled a climbing black snake. Soon they were up level with the dam. As they rode past it, Fred cast an admiring eye at the way the engineers had fitted the curving bow of the dam between the looming dark volcanic walls of the canyon. The smell of tossing blue waters was sweet.

They met several cars. Fred geared the car down to low and carefully aimed his left fender past their oncoming left fender. It was sometimes a tight fit.

"You don't shift down like I do," Miss Minerva noted.

"It's all in how you ease up on the footfeed."

"I surely wish I could learn to do that."

"You will. When you get to your brother's ranch, ask

157

him if you can't take this old Essex out in his alfalfa field, or his pasture, and try practicing there. If the field is big enough you can't hurt a thing."

They continued along an extremely narrow ledge. The overhanging granite rocks hid the sun, darkening the day. The canyon narrowed and deepened. The blue water on their left also darkened.

Miss Minerva, very edgy, touched his arm and pointed to a hamburger stand. It was across from a marked scenic point. "Pull over to that."

Fred smelled burning oil and decided it was a good idea. The stiff climb was heating up the engine.

The moment they stopped and Fred had pulled back the handbrake, Miss Minerva popped out of the car. She stood a moment catching her breath, with a hand to her chest and her dark eyes rolling. "I shall surely be happy when at last I turn into my brother's lane."

Fred felt compassion for her. "Are you all right?"

"I guess so." Then with breath caught, and nerves steady again, Miss Minerva bought them each a malted milk and a hamburger.

Fred was glad that Miss Minerva at least had a hearty appetite.

Miss Minerva went over to one side of the stand and disposed of their used paper cups and paper bags in a garbage can. On the way back she picked up a brochure. She came reading it toward the car. Something on its cover had caught her eye.

Fred stood leaning against the front fender. "What's up?"

"It says here that the traveler is well-warned the cost of food is very dear in Yellowstone Park. That the traveler is well-advised to take with him a stock of provisions."

"Tourist trap talk. It's just a scare the local leeches

158

throw at you so you'll spend your money here. Instead of up in the park."

Miss Minerva read the paragraph carefully again. "Well, they wouldn't print this information unless it were true."

"Local business men feeding off the tourist trade will tell you anything."

"Nevertheless, suppose it turns out to be true? Then it'll be too late to turn back for provisions."

"Are you any good at cookouts?"

"No, I've never cooked out." Miss Minerva sighed. "But I want to be saving too. Oh dear, isn't there some way around that dratted park to my brother's?"

"Well, actually we could've avoided the park. You saw that when I showed you the map yesterday. But it's a long way around. And you're still going to be driving through rugged country."

"That Grand Loop in the park, can't we cut that short somehow?"

"No, once you're on it, you have to take it." Fred thought a moment. "Though the Grand Loop is built like a figure 8, and we could take just the lower part of it, go around as far as the Old Faithful Geyser, and then go out through the West Entrance. That's where you take 191 west to Boise and I take 187 north to Belgrade."

"I know. You showed me." She looked at him appealingly. "Are you any good at cookouts?"

"I've done it."

"Just to be on the safe side I think I shall get us some provisions. How long do you think it'll take us to go through the park?"

"Two days."

"For two days it shall be then."

"What about a tent? The lodging'll probably be expensive too."

Miss Minerva looked at the brochure again. "It says here one can rent a canvas tent at a reasonable rate."

"Good."

While Miss Minerva went to get the groceries, Fred visited the men's privy behind the hamburger stand. It was set back into a little opening in the granite wall.

When he got back to the car he saw that Miss Minerva had bought two grocery bags of food. "Goodness, you got enough there for a small army."

"Well, we're both hearty eaters, I've discovered," she said with a little smile. "Especially in this mountain air. It invigorates one so."

"What've you all got there?"

"Eggs and smoked bacon. Bread and sandwich meat. Butter. Some oranges and apples. Head lettuce. Carrots. And two steaks for tonight."

"Steaks yet." Fred licked his lips. "Those we can broil up on some green sticks at the edge of the fire."

"That's what the man said."

Fred sniffed in the near bag. "And that smoked bacon, mmm, smells good." Fred smiled at Miss Minerva. "Well, lady, tonight when we arrive I shall build us a handsome fire. Then we'll have us a real picnic up in magic land."

Miss Minerva stowed the bags of groceries away between their suitcases on the back seat.

Fred started up the Essex and they were off.

The canyon widened and the tar road took on width. The hard rocks on their right were as polished as the stone floor of a Frisian milk room. As they climbed, the backed up waters behind the dam gradually lowered. Presently they saw the river running again, a froth of churning white on red rocks.

Weird sculptured figures began to appear on both

160

rims of the canyon. The figures reminded Fred of a picture he'd seen of the gargoyles on the Notre Dame cathedral.

Miss Minerva was fascinated by the strange rock figures. She pawed through the brochure, at last found reference to them. For the first time on the trip she became interested in the scenery. "Slow down a minute," she commanded when a particularly grotesque formation appeared high up on the skyline to their right. "That's got to be The Laughing Pig."

Fred leaned over the wheel and peered up through the windshield. He saw something that looked like a pig with its mouth open all right, but it wasn't much of a likeness. He decided to have a little fun with her. "Where?"

"Up there past that clump of pine."

"Looks more like an anteater to me."

"But look at the snout it has. It can't be an anteater."

"Well, if you stretch your imagination a little . . ."

A mile later she cried out again. "Slow down. That's got to be The Garden of the Goops."

Fred looked. There did seem to be a strange straggle of projections sticking out of the left horizon. "What's a goop?"

"A goop is a . . ." she began. "Well, I guess I don't know what a goop is."

"Ha. You can see how ridiculous that all is, seeing likenesses in those formations and then giving them names. As if they really were those things. A laughing pig. That's a lot of malarky for old school marms to get excited about. It's the kind of thing they'd call cute."

Miss Minerva was offended. "I am not an old school marm."

"The next thing you know you'll be creating idols out of them. And you know what the Good Lord has said

161

about that. 'Thou shalt have no false gods before me.'"

"Even the Devil can quote the Bible."

Fred looked up at the Garden of the Goops some more. "Well, if those are goops, then I'm not sure if I ever want to meet any. They all look like human monsters to me. Worse even then gorillas." Fred remembered that Ma had once given birth to a funny looking baby. It had lived for only an hour. Uncle Hank had made a small box for it and buried it in the Hillside Cemetery. "Like a child born with a waterhead."

Miss Minerva shuddered. "Och. You do have the awful habit of always saying the most shocking things."

It wasn't long before she spotted another figure. She studied it carefully, checked her brochure, finally announced, "That's got to be The Goose."

Fred had a look. "Looks more like an anvil to me."

"Well, it looks like a goose to me. And that's what it is."

Fred shook his head.

And it wasn't long before she found yet another likeness. She held up the brochure and glanced from the likeness to the brochure and back again. "I'm sure that's what it is."

"What is?"

"Something you shouldn't have much trouble recognizing," she said snappish. "The Devil's Elbow."

By straining one's imagination a little the odd rock formation did resemble an elbow all right. "Lady, from where I sit that could just as well be a stovepipe elbow."

"Nevermind. Just let me have my fun for once."

Fred fell silent. It was true. She hadn't enjoyed the trip much so far.

A few miles farther along she found another resemblance. "And that's got to be Thor's Anvil."

Fred made it a point not to look. A short distance up

162

ahead the narrow road was turning to gravel again.

Several winding turns more and Miss Minerva found yet another likeness. "Now there's one you can't help but make out," she said briskly.

Fred looked. "Say." She was right. It did suggest something concrete. "Four fellows sitting on a sled."

"Right. They call it Four Old Men On A Toboggan."

"A very interesting accident of nature."

"Och!" Miss Minerva snapped her brochure shut. "You're a spoilsport." She turned slightly away from him and stared out at the passing scenery.

Gradually the tossing landscape filled with evergreens.

Oncoming cars trailed yellow plumes of dust, through which Fred sometimes had to drive almost half-blinded. Soon a car came up behind them very fast. The driver didn't care to eat the Essex's dust for very long and sought for an opening, a straight level stretch, in which to pass.

Fred stared at the fellow in his rearview mirror. "Damned tailgater."

"No swearing please."

"I ought to teach him a lesson."

"Nevermind him now. This is my car and you just drive as if he weren't there."

The road straightened out for an eighth of a mile and the car following them suddenly shot past them in a blast of billowing yellow dust. The car was a Packard and the man driver and his female companion were flashily dressed. For a few seconds Fred had trouble seeing where the road was.

"Good riddance," Miss Minerva said.

"Perfumed big shots," Fred muttered. "I'll bet a buck they think their farts don't stink."

Miss Minerva was shocked. "Really. Such language. If you drive for me much longer I'm just going to have to wash out your mouth."

Fred gave that thought the once-over and then started to laugh right outloud. "Now that's something I'd like to see. You wrestling me to the ground and then trying to wash out my mouth. That'd be a sight for sore eyes." Fred laughed some more. "Because right in the middle of it all, I'd reach up and give you a kiss."

Miss Minerva stiffened in her seat. "You — would — not!"

"That's what I'd do with my mother. Get her to laugh."

"No one's ever kissed me. And I'm surely not going to begin by letting you kiss me. A stranger."

"You wouldn't want a nice little Fred kiss from me?"

She got mad. "You young kids, always got sex on the brain. Sex maniacs."

An opening appeared ahead in the forest. A brown signboard with yellow lettering swung into view:

First Ranger Station In The United States
Erected 1903-4

Beyond the sign stood a large brown-painted building with a spacious parking lot. A green ranger pickup stood near the front door. A thin plume of smoke rose from a single chimney.

They passed through Wapiti. The highway kept rising. Ears cracked; cleared; cracked some more. Nostrils cracked too. The forests of pine and spruce and fir thickened and became taller by the mile. There were great throws of mountain slopes black with timber. Smell of clean moss wafted in through the open window. Breathing thin high mountain air Fred had the feeling he was getting healthier by the minute.

They came upon another brown sign with yellow lettering:

SHOSHONE NATIONAL FOREST
The First National Forest In The United States
March 30, 1891

Ears really began to crack. Fred had to swallow and swallow, and shake his head, to clear them. There were times when the old Essex motor seemed to run as silent as an electric car; then as loud as a noisy old truck with the cutout open. Miss Minerva kept whacking the side of her head, first over the right ear and then over the left ear, to get her hearing back.

Fred cocked an ear at the engine. He wondered if he'd set the choke closed enough. The carburetor was making a sucking noise and the engine didn't have as much power as before.

The forest wall on either side of the road became taller and thicker. The pungent odor of fresh pine needles filled their car. Springs tumbled everywhere, on both sides of the highway, forming little streams in the roadside ditches. Water smelled different that high up.

"Beautiful," Fred murmured over the wheel, driving carefully at the same time that he was trying to take everything in, "spectacular. Now I'm glad I came. Man. Makes me want to get out and start jumping from one mountain peak to another."

Miss Minerva was beginning to look scared again.

"Give me a pair of wings no bigger than a hummingbird's and I could take off."

Miss Minerva's fingers twisted through each other like garter snakes in mating season. "Heights scare me so. Especially in strange places."

The old Essex Super Six pounded heavily up past Eagle Creek and Sleeping Giant. Pahaska, a little settlement of stores and a gas station, showed up ahead in a clearing. It was around three and the sun cast sharp purple shadows halfway across the main store.

Fred read aloud some white lettering in the store window:

> "Last chance to buy meat, bread,
> vegetables, fruit cheap, it pays to camp out
> in the park!"

Fred turned to Miss Minerva. "Looks like we could've also bought our supplies here."

Miss Minerva stared at the lettering too, though she was reading the prices, "Yes. But oh are they dear."

They continued to climb. The old engine gave off an old oil stink. And Miss Minerva began to exude an odor too. Her smell was almost pleasant: a hint of tar soap, a hint of musk. It was the way Ma's muff used to smell. Fred wondered if Miss Minerva had also begun to smell him. He hadn't changed clothes for several days.

Traffic thickened. Fred followed four cars around a winding turn.

Soon a little green booth appeared beside a gateway. A ranger dressed in green with a peaked hat held up a hand and stopped each car as it approached him. Fred pulled up behind the line. They'd reached the entrance to the great park.

Miss Minerva looked at a sign behind the ranger. "It says something about an entrance fee. Oh dear, then it is going to cost us to go through the park."

The cars moved ahead one by one. Soon they were close enough to make out the price.

"Two-fifty!" Miss Minerva whispered sharply.

"I'll pay it if you want me to. I want to see the park."

Miss Minerva was tempted to accept the offer; at last said. "No, you're doing such a good job driving in the mountains I better pay for it."

"We'll make up for that two-fifty tonight when we camp out."

"We better," Miss Minerva said. She began to fumble through her purse.

Fred pulled up even with the ranger.

"Greetings," the ranger said, leaning down into the car on Fred's side. "Welcome to Yellowstone National Park." The ranger was a slim vigorous looking fellow, with a pinkish-brown face and lively brown eyes. His brown eyes seemed to look everywhere at once both in the front and the back seats. He spotted the food. "Be careful you do not feed the bears. It may seem cute to see a bear eat an apple or a doughnut, but if he should happen to demand more, he can be very dangerous."

"How much is the entrance fee?" Miss Minerva asked.

"Just like it says up there. Two-fifty for each car."

"Then it doesn't matter how many are in a car?"

"No." Other tourists were pulling up behind the Essex. One of the drivers honked. The ranger waved at the driver to be patient.

Miss Minerva held her purse tight against her belly, barely open, and fingered out three dollar bills. She handed them to Fred who handed them on to the ranger.

The ranger handed back fifty cents in change. He leaned down once more and pointed a lean arm ahead. "You'll shortly be going up through Sylvan Pass. They had some snow up there last night so it's apt to be a bit slushy. Drive carefully and you'll be all right. The snow is melting and there are tracks in the wet snow. Just follow the tracks."

"Thanks."

They drove on. It wasn't long before their ears began to crack loud again. The road narrowed and curled up around stiff slopes. The fir and spruce appeared to have been stabbed into the slopes to make them stick. The valley on their left began to open off into a vast long serpentine chasm. A couple of times the old engine coughed, missed, caught again. Fred held his breath. Miss Minerva cocked her ear at the motor too.

The road kept lifting, lifting, curving up and around, and finally, around yet another turn, snow showed up. It was wet heavy snow and it shone dully in the slanting sunlight.

"Now that's the first time I ever saw snow in August," Fred whispered.

It was like driving in a dream. Their ears were momentarily stuffed shut so that the car ran silently, at the same time that their nostrils were wide open to the smell of wet rosin.

The driver up ahead wandered out of the tracks in the snow and for a few rods his rear wheels kicked up slush all over the Essex windshield. In a second Fred's view was plakked shut.

Quickly, cussing under his breath, Fred worked the wipers and cleared out halfmoons of vision for them. "Dumb bastard," Fred whispered to himself.

At last they came to the crest. At the same moment their ears cracked clear. The cracking in their ears had the effect of an extra shutter being opened in their eyes.

The view ahead was the most dazzling Fred had ever seen. The Big Horns had been a marvel, but the vast expanse below them, and the far reaches out to the north and out to the south, were greater. Immediately below them spread one of the bluest lakes Fred had ever seen, bluer by far than Lake Michigan. Up from its edges rose ridge after ridge of glistening evergreens.

"Watch where you're going!" Miss Minerva cried.

Fred jerked the wheel over. Like the driver ahead earlier, Fred had wandered out of the tracks too and was kicking up slush on the car behind. "Sorry." Fred shook his head. "I'll bet they've had accidents here."

Miss Minerva saw where the road veered around a corner off into nowhere. "Oh dear Lord."

"Don't worry. We'll make it or know the reason why."

"I can't wait to get down below there."

The road headed toward the northwest, banking and curving. Then it began to drop rapidly. Soon the engine began to purr smoothly again. Ears kept cracking the other way, and sometimes they heard their motor and sometimes they didn't. Magpies scolded at the passing cars. The red cut in the right wall bled red springs. The cars began to pull away from each other as the drivers gained confidence. Presently the snow was gone and they were back in a drifting green world. The blue lake off to their left lay ruffled under a north breeze. It cast up millions of momentary mirrors.

A tumbling tune started up in Fred's head. It was the same one he'd once heard while watching Special Face walk across the campus at Calvin. That part of his self-welling internal spring had been dry for a spell. The tune seemed to have nine notes, all of them whole, like those in a Dutch psalm. On a staff they'd have resembled two mountain peaks set close together.

Head cocked to one side, Fred listened to his internal maker. The nine-note phrase was being played several ways on a dozen moaning violins, first the twin peaks were being counterpointed with twin valleys, then they were being restructured into a mountain range of co-

169

lumnar harmony. A symphony. It was much more clear to him as to shape and thrust than anything he'd ever envisioned in writing. He'd read many novels; had often wondered how a Tolstoy or a Melville had drawn their epics out of their being; and couldn't conceive of how he'd fill three hundred plus pages when it came time for him to write his novel. But in music, there he'd —

"What's wrong with you?"

"Who? Me?"

"You were looking so funny at the road. Did you see something?"

Fred had learned long ago not to tell people what he sometimes heard in his head. They'd give him a look as though they thought him crazy. "It was nothing. Just thinking to myself."

"Well, I was going to say."

The road continued to sink; the mountainside on their right continued to rise. They followed the north shore of the deep blue lake, until crossing a little bridge, they entered the Fishing Bridge Campground. Under scattered tall pines stood various buildings: a long brown cafeteria, garage and repair shop, picture shops, housekeeping cabins, bathhouse and laundry, and a single row of canvas tents. The windshields of several hundred cars blinked in a parking lot. Despite the hundreds of tourists wandering about, the camp ground area was very neat.

The sun was almost down. The top of the mountain ridge to west hurled long purple-green shadows at them. The bracing smell of crushed needles entered the car.

Fred pulled up in front of the information center. "Well, lady, I told you we'd make it."

Miss Minerva let out a woman's wonderful sigh.

"You want me to find us a cabin?"

Miss Minerva quickly got hold of herself. She

clutched her purse. "No, I'll make the arrangements. You just stay near the car. And watch out for the bears." She got out and went over to talk to the ranger in the information center.

Fred got out too and stretched. It'd been another long day behind the wheel. He slowly turned, heels squinching on the gravel, eyes taking in the sights. He stretched again. He filled his chest with the sweet green air; breathed deep until he was almost drunk.

Miss Minerva appeared to be having some trouble getting what she wanted. Fred wandered over. The ranger was middle-aged, face lined with weather marks, green uniform freshly pressed, brown shoes polished to mirrors.

"A cabin is really that much," Miss Minerva said, biting on her lips. "Well then, how much are the tents?"

"One dollar a night."

"Are they safe from animals?"

"Just be sure to leave your food in the car. And make sure the car is locked."

"Can we have a look at the tents?"

"Right over there."

Miss Minerva led the way, Fred following. They walked up a path past some log cabins, then turned right toward a row of tents. The tents were part-cabins. The roofs were made of green-painted wood and the walls of a heavy green duck canvas. Miss Minerva selected one of better looking tents at the far end. She peeked inside; backed out with a sour grimace.

Fred waited her pleasure.

Miss Minerva finally made up her mind. "Well, I'll just have to take it." She looked at the number over the canvas flap door. "Twenty-two. I've already spent more here than I planned on. That entrance fee I hadn't expected. Now I've got to save that back."

"A dollar a tent isn't much. I'll pay for my own."

"No, no, you've worked hard and I mean to pay for all your expenses so long as you're driving for me."

"Really though, I'm willing to pay a dollar for a tent. One dollar isn't going to break me."

"No, no. I don't want you to spend any money so long as you're working for me. No, what we'll do is I'll sleep in the tent and you sleep in the car. Every dollar adds up, you know."

"That it does." Fred was thinking of the dollar in his billfold and the five bills tucked in his shoe. But he didn't like the idea of sleeping in her car too well.

They walked back to the ranger. Miss Minerva paid for one tent as well as for a permit to build a campfire. Fred drove the car around the single row of roofed tents and parked it just outside the doorway of No. 22. Miss Minerva got out her suitcase as well as the two packages of food while Fred quickly scurried out under the thick pines and gathered up a small armful of sticks and twigs. He set the sticks up into the shape of a tepee and lit a fire under them.

"What a strange way to arrange the firewood," Miss Minerva commented.

"Get the quickest heat that way," Fred said. "Learned that from an old trapper back home. I used to run into him along the river having a cookout by himself."

Miss Minerva spread out a blue tablecloth on the duff near the fire. She set out bread, butter, vegetables, steaks, oranges, apples.

Fred got out his jackknife and cut them each a green stick. He speared the green sticks into the steaks and then set the green sticks at an angle into the ground near the fire. It took but a minute for the fat on the steaks to begin sizzling. It was but another minute and the smell of broiling meat was sweet on the air. Fred watched the

172

steaks carefully, turning them as needed.

"How do you want yours?" he asked.

"Well-done."

"Two well-dones coming up."

Several other cars pulled up alongside the tents down the line. All were families out on vacation. Soon they too had cookout fires going. Meanwhile the log cabins were being rapidly filled up. Most of the latecomers went over to the cafeteria to eat.

Fred became aware that Miss Minerva had fallen very silent. He looked up to find her staring at something behind him. Fred slowly turned around still sitting on his heels. Well, there they were. Two cinnamon bears. Fred was surprised to see how small they were. They were hardly bigger than Pa's old dog Rover. One of the bears was rampant and eagerly sniffing the air. The other had his head down low as though intending to dart in and snatch up some of their supper.

Fred said over his shoulder, "Don't move. They won't hurt us." Fred was quite pleased to discover he wasn't a bit afraid of them. Farm boys were rarely afraid of animals, tame or wild.

Miss Minerva drew in a slow breath.

"Bears are only overgrown dogs," Fred said.

"Throw them something to eat so they'll go away," Miss Minerva whispered.

"Now that's exactly what we're not going to do. That'll really make them hungry for our steaks."

The family next down the line spotted the bears too. They sat frozen, eyes like moons.

Fred turned over the steaks one more time and then casually got to his feet. He took several slow steps toward the cinnamon bears; then, of a sudden, threw out his arms and jumped toward them, at the same time letting go with a great roaring "Rrrror-acch!" The two

173

little bears were dumbfounded; and broke, tumbling over each other in their hurry to get away. They scudded away in a hard gallop and disappeared over a rise.

Everybody up and down the line of tents laughed in relief.

Miss Minerva also allowed herself a little smile. "Wherever did you get the nerve to do that? Goodness."

"Watching my father handle castastrophes on the farm."

"Well I never."

Fred examined the steaks closely. "I think, your ladyship, your steak is ready."

Miss Minerva was all attention. She dug into her grocery bags and came up with two paper plates. She set them on the ground near Fred.

Fred neatly, with a little fancy flourish like Uncle Hank might do, placed the largest steak in Miss Minerva's plate and the smaller steak in his plate.

Miss Minerva licked her lips. "It smells so good. If I wasn't famished before I surely am now."

Fred was getting a little sick of that word famished. It was going to be one word he was not going to enter in his little black word-book.

"Oh dear. The next question is going to be, how are we going to cut our steaks? These little tin forks I got with the groceries won't help much."

With the knowing smile of an old camper, Fred got out his jackknife again and opened the longest sharpest blade.

"You're not going to use that, are you?"

"Why not?"

"The Lord only knows what you've used it for. Besides cutting those green sticks."

"Such as?"

"Cutting all those smelly things on the farm."

174

"Including apples and watermelons. And afterwards always wiped clean on one's pants."

"Ugh."

Fred swung half-around and momentarily held the blade in the little licking orange flames. "That should purify the blade. Not even a queen can complain now." Fred deftly cut his steak into small chunks. The blade was very sharp. He handed the knife over to Miss Minerva. "And if there was any doubt the blade wasn't clean, it should be all wiped off on my portion. Okay?"

Miss Minerva took the knife between thumb and forefinger. Her upper lip wrinkled back under her nose. At last, overcoming her squeamishness, she took a firm grip on the bonehandle and cut her steak into manageable chunks too. Then she settled herself on a stump as though she were at a state banquet.

Between bites, Fred said, "I have to hand it to you though, Miss Minerva. No matter how hungry you are, you always manage to remain the mannered lady."

Miss Minerva gave him a wrinkling look. "Now you're trying to butter me up."

"Well, a biscuit you're not. So if it's butter I have for you, it must be for something else."

"Now what do you mean by that."

A gulp of laughter escaped Fred. "Well now, that I wouldn't know myself."

The steak was great. So were the vegetables and the bread and butter.

The tourist children further down the line were having a grand time, skirling around the picnic fires with their happy birdlike voices, laughing in mock disobedience to their mothers' clucking calls, playing tag, now and then darting in for a bite of food.

Fred was the first to see it. He was facing toward the thickest part of the forest away from the lake, and was

175

really thinking about nothing much except eating, when the back part of his brain spotted something in the shadows. The something was darker than the shadows. Then, even as he opened a full look at it, the shadow enlarged, became the great broad head and the wide dark shoulders of a black bear, and came straight for them. Fred felt a tight little pinching motion in his belly for a second, but then, before it could grab him and stiffen him in his tracks, he moved. He set his plate to one side and stood up.

Miss Minerva saw the huge black thing then too. Her mouth opened. A series of little squeaking sounds came out of it.

"Shh," Fred shushed. "Shut up. Don't let him hear how scared you are."

Miss Minerva shut up.

The other families were suddenly silent too. The children hurried to their mothers. The fathers took up protective positions at the head of their fires.

The black bear kept coming in a deliberate shambling gate, swinging its huge head from side to side as its nose tracked the scent of singed meat.

Fred looked around for a club of some sort.

A dozen feet away the bear rose up on its hind legs.

Fred was startled to see that the bear was taller than he was. Fred wondered how good a boxer the bear might be up on two legs. The bear should be just a little teetery on two legs. Back in college Jack Brouwer had taught Fred how to feint and then counter with a short powerful right-cross to the nose.

It never came to that. There was a piercing whistle behind them.

Fred whirled around.

It was the ranger from the information center. He'd come up and blown an animal trainer's whistle.

176

The whistle was magic. The black bear shook his head, hard, several times, as if he couldn't stand the high piercing noise; then dropped to earth and turned and tumbled off into the dark shadows of the forest again.

"Mercy stars alive," Miss Minerva whispered.

Fred gave the ranger a smile of relief. "Thanks for coming up."

The ranger smiled in return, his weathered face wrinkling up. "That was our old friend Black Bimbo. He likes to come around about this time of the day and throw a scare into people. He's run off with a lot of people's steaks. He's one of the few bears around who likes his steaks well-done. About the only raw meat he cares for is smoked bacon."

"Oh dear," Miss Minerva said.

The ranger glanced down at her. "You have some smoked bacon with you?"

"Yes. I thought we could have some for breakfast tomorrow morning."

The ranger pursed his lips in thought. "Smoked bacon they can smell through a cement wall. More so than pure raw meat. Perhaps you'd better bring it over to my office. I have an icebox and it'll be safe there."

"We'll think about it," Miss Minerva said.

"Don't say I didn't warn you."

Fred held up a hand. "Sir, I was just thinking . . . Miss Baxter says I can sleep in her car tonight, but I think I'd rather sleep on the duff under the trees. Do you think it'll be safe?"

"I wouldn't advise it. Though around here the bears usually don't bother people. Over at the Old Faithful Lodge there's grizzlies and they are dangerous."

"Thanks. I'll just have to suffer it sitting up then."

The ranger moved on, stopping to chat with the other

177

families down the line.

As the sun sank into the rumpled horizon the shadows rose under the trees. Smoke from the little fires diffused through the purple shadows. The smells were comforting, spitting pine knots, drying rosin, seared lichen.

For dessert Miss Minerva served them each an apple and an orange.

When they'd finished, Fred got some water and put out the fire while Miss Minerva put what was left of the food back into her grocery bags.

Fred stretched and yawned. "Before I turn in I think I'll take me a little walk."

"Where you going?" she asked suspicious.

"I thought I'd like to take a peek at Fishing Bridge there. And then maybe go over to the cafeteria and see how the rich are living it up."

"You're not satisfied with what you have with me?"

"Oh, Miss Minerva, don't be that way. I just want to see the sights. Look, if you want me to, I'll bring that package of smoked bacon over to the ranger. For him to put in his icebox."

Her lips worked as though she were trying to dislodge a tiny piece of meat caught in her teeth. "I'll take care of the smoked bacon. Don't worry."

"Have it your way. But don't lock the car. I'll be along shortly."

Fred first went over to the information center and got himself a map of the park. He studied it in the falling light. "I've got to make sure that we take the lower part of the Grand Loop as far as the Old Faithful Geyser. That way we'll see the most important sights. Plus the grizzly bears."

Fred walked out onto Fishing Bridge. Several anglers had a line out. Leaning over the peeled log railing, Fred

178

watched marvelously clear water slowly flowing under him. Looking south past a point of trees, Fred spotted the great body of water he'd seen earlier and which the map said was Yellowstone Lake. There was no wind out and in the evening dusk the surface of the lake shone like patent leather. A strange bird sang a last evening song.

"God, if only Special Face were here. It's all so beautiful I think it would work on her enough to make her fall in love with me."

He next strolled toward the cafeteria and store. The building was of rock and concrete columns made to resemble hewn logs. Fred wondered what possessed the architect to make one thing resemble another. If it was to look like it was made of logs, why not real logs? And if a rock and cement effect was wanted, why not straight rock and cement? A tree in cement clothing. It wasn't honest.

The inside of the cafeteria he liked better, especially the rock fireplace, with a little fire burning in it. The fireplace was so huge he could step into it without touching the arch. The ceiling too was lovely, high smoked rafters supported by pillars of local rock.

Fishing Bridge Museum he liked best of all. It was one-story high and made of peeled timbers and rock pillars. There was nothing like having a building made of local materials. It reminded him of Luverne in Minnesota. A good share of Luverne's buildings were made of beautiful purple Sioux quartzite quarried in the nearby Blue Mounds. The lighting fixtures inside the Fishing Bridge Museum were decorated with antlers. He paused to study some of the displays, flora and fauna of the park, geological formations, and Indian artifacts. The museum was half-full of tourists, staring, reading, musing.

179

It was dark and quite chilly when Fred headed back to Miss Minerva's Essex. He found her canvas door latched shut. She'd gone to bed. Careful not to disturb her, he turned the handle of the car door and got in. It took him a while to find a comfortable position. He rustled out his red blanket from his suitcase and tucked it under his lower back and then hung his long legs up over the steering wheel. It was almost a fetal crouch and it was all right. The worst was he knew that every now and then during the night he'd feel the urge to stretch himself straight out, from the two moons in his hair to his two big toes, and in that cramped position wouldn't be able to do it.

He wondered if he shouldn't have knocked on Miss Minerva's tent door to ask if she'd brought the smoked bacon to the ranger's icebox. She might just have been afraid enough of the evening shadows not to do it. He sniffed around inside the car to see if she'd tucked it under their suitcases. But he couldn't detect any smoked meat smell. Wouldn't it be something if she'd left the smoked bacon in the car though, and big old Black Bimbo decided he wanted it? Fred wondered if Black Bimbo was strong enough to break a car window. Or tip the Essex over on its side. He'd heard of grizzlies who'd been strong enough to scatter a pile of telephone poles as though they were toothpicks, all to find a rabbit hidden under them.

He loosened his tie and nuzzled his chin down inside his shirt collar. The opened shirt released some of his body smells. He thought the smell rather pleasant: clean flesh, a touch of some kind of soap, and a soft yeasty male odor. Of course everybody thought his own body smells weren't half bad. Even a fellow who smelled like old rancid buttermilk still thought he smelled all right.

It got stuffy inside the car. Sleepily, he crooked a

hand behind himself and rolled down the window a tiny crack. Ah, that was better. Chill air breathed over his hair, ruffling a tuft or two. In a moment he was breathing it. It tasted as good as cool fresh rainwater.

The campground had fallen silent. The pines overhead rustled in the night breeze. Once a child cried out in dream.

Fred wondered what Special Face might be doing right that minute. Probably kissing the other fellow.

Fred wondered how Miss Minerva was getting along. She was probably curled up into a tight squirrel of a ball on her cot. Because of the night chill she'd probably kept on most of her clothes as well as piled on the blankets.

He was just drifting off to sleep when he heard it. A cautious padding of heavy feet. A slow deep sniffing of the air. A twig cracked. Yes, a brain was sending out its feelers to see where everybody was sleeping. After a second Fred felt those alien brain feelers within a foot his head. If it wasn't a camp thief it had to be big Black Bimbo. Probably checking out the car for the smoked bacon. The hair all over Fred's back ruffed up. There were several slowly drawn snuffs immediately behind Fred's head. Apparently satisfied the smoked bacon wasn't in the Essex, the searching brain backed away from the car.

Fred relaxed a little.

There was some more cautious rustling nearby. The black brain was sniffing over the ashes. Then the black brain retreated into the woods and there were no more sounds.

Gradually Fred nodded off to sleep. He dreamt he was sitting in a big wooden swing and that Pa was trying to give him a push but no matter how hard Pa tried he couldn't budge the swing. It had the brakes on and the two ropes just would not bend. Pa gave the whole thing another look, the stiff swing and the big cottonwood tree it was tied to, and made up his mind. He put his arms around the huge cottonwood and with a mighty wrenching heave tore the tree out of the earth, roots and all, and then, with another mighty wrenching motion, threw everything, with Fred still in the swing, into an enormous canyon. Fred hung onto the swing for dear life. But when Fred saw where he was going to land, in the great red mouth of Black Bimbo the bear, he —

There was a terrified shriek.

Fred jerked upright, cracking his head against the roof of the car.

There was another shriek, this time even louder, of both terror and outrage.

Miss Minerva. Something had happened to her. Fred already knew what it was. He lifted his legs off the steering wheel and bounced out of the car. He was just in time to see, in the vague light under the trees coming from the parking area, the huge burly hairy form of something black galloping off into the dark with an odd-looking object in its teeth.

Miss Minerva continued to shriek, shrill on quavering shrill. The shriek radiated out of her tent like the whistle of a siren.

Everybody came rushing out of their tent doors, half-dressed, hair wild, mouths open. "What happened?"

The park ranger on duty in the Information Center came on the dead run carrying a rifle, "What's going on out here?"

Fred pointed at Miss Minerva's tent. One side of it appeared to have been deftly rolled up in a couple of feet while the other side had been blasted out with the staked ends flipped back over on its log roof.

"My God." The ranger jerked a long flashlight off a

182

hook on his belt and flicked it on and aimed its beam of light through the blasted tent.

There on her back lay Miss Minerva in her nightgown on the floor, bare legs up in the air and pumping like she was in a furious bicycle race. Her eyes were tight shut and her mouth was wide open. Her shrieks continued to fracture the night air. The ranger worked his flashlight quickly through the tent, but not finding any culprits next flashed it all around outside, far out under the pines and then up and down the line of tents.

Fred said, "I think it was that big black bear we saw earlier in the evening. The other ranger called him Black Bimbo."

"Yeh," the night duty ranger said. "There was a note on my desk about that. Miss Baxter never did bring in her smoked bacon."

"I was afraid of that." Fred settled on his heels and called into the tent. "Miss Minerva?"

Miss Minerva continued to shriek and pedal the air. The ranger said, "She's hysterical."

"Yeh." Fred noticed the double ring of faces that had gathered around them, staring, mouths agape. "Get back, you people. This is private."

"Not if a bear did that, it ain't," an older man said.

Fred crawled inside the tent. He placed his hand firmly on Miss Minerva's belly. "Now now. Quiet down here. It ain't all that bad."

She paused, gathered breath, eyes opening very wide and white. She saw his silhouette; promptly pinched shut her eyes again and cried out. "I knew it, I knew it!"

"Oh shut up, Miss Minerva." Fred gave her a rough shake. "Everything's all right. You're still alive and that's all that matters."

Again she fell silent. "Frederick?"

"Yes, Miss Minerva, it's me, your driver. Come, get yourself up off that floor."

She jerked erect. "Where's my bathrobe?"

The light from the ranger's flashlight fell on a chair over which she'd draped her clothes. The cot she'd slept on was tumbled over on its side, partially collapsed, with one of the blankets pulled partway outside. Fred spotted a red-and-black robe. "Here you are."

Stiffly she got to her feet and slipped into her bathrobe. Then she opened her tent from the inside and stepped outside. When she spotted all the gaping faces in the wavering light she turned sideways to them. "Mercy me."

The ranger aimed his flashlight around at all the faces. "Okay, you can all go back to bed. Everything's under control here." He had the alert face and erect stance of an athlete.

Not one face left.

The ranger took Miss Minerva by the arm. "Are you all right?"

"Of course I'm all right. Though I didn't think so a minute ago when that monster almost raped me."

"What happened?"

"Well, I was sound asleep, dreaming about my brother and how nice it would be to see him again, when all of a sudden I awoke feeling myself being lifted up in the air as if an earthquake were erupting under me. When I threw out my hands to save myself, I felt all this hair. I thought sure Frederick my driver here had come to rape me. Och!"

"My God, Miss Baxter," Fred cried.

"Well, I did. And considering everything, how was I to know? I know nothing about what makes you men such animals."

"Me, of all people?"

185

The ranger broke, in. "Then what happened?"

"Well, then the next thing I knew this hairy beast got his nose between the mattress and the cot and proceeded to pass between the two."

The ranger gave her a sideways look. "You put some food under your mattress, didn't you?"

Miss Minerva went on the attack. "What kind of a park do you people run here, letting wild animals get in among civilized people." Miss Minerva flexed herself up on her toes. "And so what if I did decide to hide my bacon under my mattress? Isn't that my privilege in America? It's a free country, isn't it, where I keep my bacon?"

The ranger almost smiled. He said politely, "Weren't you warned about the bears when you drove into the park?"

"Well, I certainly wasn't told about bears wanting to get into bed with one."

"And wasn't it suggested that you should place your bacon in our icebox for safekeeping?"

"Well, I thought my bacon would be perfectly safe where I put it. And anyway, I tied my tent shut and that should have been safe enough, and if it wasn't, then you shouldn't be allowed to rent people tents around bears, but should have only secure log cabins with steel locks."

Fred smiled. "Well, anyway, Miss Minerva, everything's turned out all right in the end, hasn't it? What's important is that you're safe. So why don't we all go to bed and get in some sleep. Okay?"

"But my bacon? What'll we have for breakfast?"

Fred took her firmly by the arm. "I'll buy us a breakfast in the cafeteria in the morning. Come, let's go to bed. I'll help you tie down the sides of your tent."

The young ranger thought that was a good idea. He waved his flashlight at the other campers again. "All

186

right, everything's under control. You can go back to bed now."

There was some muttering about the danger of wild bears, and several of the men campers stood talking a moment, but soon everybody went to bed.

Fred and the ranger put Miss Minerva's cot back together again, and restaked the sides of her tent, and comforted her with joshing small talk until, with several clucking sighs, Miss Minerva got back on her cot.

Fred was wide awake and he walked with the ranger part way back to the Information Center. "Thanks a lot."

"All part of a night's work."

"She's sure some dame."

"She relation of yours?"

"No. We just met a couple of days ago. I was hitchhiking in South Dakota and she picked me up. She needed a driver."

The young ranger became alert. "She doesn't know you very well then?"

"No, nor I her. And I'll be glad when our ways part."

"Well, aren't you free to leave her any time you want to?"

"I suppose I am." Fred scuffed at the gravel in the path. "But you see, sir, she's a lousy driver. Until a week ago she'd never driven a car and then all of sudden she bought that Essex in Chicago and started driving west to see her brother in Boise. Man, I don't know if you noticed it or not, but she's got driving instructions pasted up on her windshield and she doesn't make a move without referring to it — even in the middle of traffic. Or, as she once did up in the Big Horns, on a curving turn near Muddy Pass! I thought for sure we were goners until I took the wheel away from her."

"Oh."

"So, even though I'm getting awfully sick of her being so bossy, I thought I'd stick with her until I got her safely into Idaho."

"Where you going?"

"I've got a friend living up in Belgrade. That's west of Bozeman there."

"Hmm." The young ranger slowly allowed himself a smile. "Well, I don't envy you. But it's pretty swell of you to take her under your wing like that."

Fred smiled. "All part of a night's work. Especially if you've been raised right."

"Yeh, I suppose. Well, good-night."

"Night."

Fred went back to the old Essex and draped his legs over the steering wheel once more and nuzzled around on the front seat until he found his old position. He laughed a couple of times as he replayed in his mind what had happened. Once he laughed right outloud, merrily, when he recalled Miss Minerva's remark that, upon feeling all that hair, she thought it was her driver Frederick come to rape her. She sure must've had some racy thoughts about him if she thought he'd have that kind of hair on him somewhere.

Fred slept.

VIII

The banging of tin cans awoke Fred. Dawn had come. Blinking, Fred spotted at the far end of the clearing two cinnamon bears nosing through garbage cans.

It was time to get up. Fred awakened Miss Minerva. When one of their neighbor campers offered them several slices of bacon, which they'd just bought up at the cafeteria, it was decided Miss Minerva would fry them bacon and eggs if Fred would scrounge up some more kindling.

They ate heartily in the crisp morning air. Both were famished. Then they cleaned up camp, paid the outdoor privies a visit, washed up in chill water Fred got from the sparkling stream near Fishing Bridge, and loaded their gear into the car.

Fred got behind the wheel and they were off. Nothing was said about the previous night. But it was not forgotten. A coolness had set in between them. Fred ached to be rid of her at the same time that he hungered to see more of the marvels of Yellowstone National Park. Miss Minerva nursed her own ambivalencies.

They followed the Yellowstone River north through groves of spindly lodgepole pine. Off on the right the jagged rim of the Absaroke Peaks lifted out of long lazy slopes of green pine. A sign pointed to a site marked Mud Volcano but Fred decided to roll on by. They couldn't stop and look at everything. There wasn't time enough. Best to save the stops for the big things.

Presently the river on their right began to descend into Hayden Valley. The water churned down through rocky cascades. It ruffed up around huge black boulders.

Dragon's Mouth came up. That sounded interesting.

"Would you like to see that?"

Miss Minerva nodded. "If you want."

Fred pulled out of the traffic and parked against a row of neatly placed stones.

Both got out of the car. A sign pointed to a hole in the nearby rock wall. The hole had the look of the wide open mouth of a snake, raw, red. An irregular hissing roar issued from it. The sign said the roar was caused by water splashing against the wall of a deep underground cave.

Another car pulled up beside the Essex. It was very shiny and it immediately caught Fred's eye. A Rolls-Royce. There was a wizened chauffer up front and what looked like father, mother, and daughter in back. Fred glanced at the license plate. It was foreign. British.

The chauffeur turned off the motor while the three in back got out. The man was quite tall, with a slight hint of a potbelly almost hidden by good tailoring, a round pink face with a pink balding head and keen blue eyes. The woman was also tall, frail-looking until one noticed the chin. The chin jutted out a little and gave her a look of iron determination. The young girl was also special: slim, very blond, quiet blue eyes, soft lips, good chin, beautiful shaped legs. All three read the sign silently, then turned for a slow laconic look at the hissing Dragon's Mouth.

The man finally spoke. "'Stroid'nary."

The woman nodded. "Very much so."

The young girl said nothing. She smiled a little, and then, quite at ease, looked Fred right in the eye. She held his look a moment and then, still at ease, looked his long body up and down.

Fred had the feeling that she belonged to some horsey set somewhere, that she knew how to read horseflesh. Further, she knew how to read him.

190

Miss Minerva caught the exchange of looks. She began to ruffle through her purse. "Frederick, what time do you have?"

Fred glanced at his wristwatch. "Going on nine."

"I think it's time we moved on. That is, if we plan to make the lower part of the Grand Loop in one day. Get to the Old Faithful Inn by nightfall."

Reluctantly Fred climbed back into the Essex. He would have liked to talk to the English girl.

The road climbed a slope of sagebrush and turned into an oblong valley surrounded by pine-covered hills. Here at last was the true Garden of Eden. Everything was a vivid green or blue. A slow river meandered down through the lower sloughs. Two dark moose were feeding in the succulent river grasses, one of them almost submerged in the water, with only its strange angular backbone showing.

Miss Minerva liked the valley. "Now here I wouldn't mind living. If my brother had a ranch in a place like this, I'd never leave."

Fred noticed in his rearview mirror that the English family in their Rolls-Royce were following them about a half mile back.

A large brown sign with sharp yellow lettering appeared around a turn on the left:

Grand Canyon Grizzly Bear Feeding Grounds.

"Hey," Fred said, "grizzlies. Them I got to see. That alone'll be worth the price of admission."

Miss Minerva gave him a black look. "But I paid our price of admission and I don't care to see them."

"But they're the king of beasts in America. Like the lion is in Africa."

"I do not wish to see them."

191

Fred rose a little in his blood. "Why not? Don't be a spoilsport."

"Didn't that ranger say that grizzlies are dangerous?"

"What does your folder there say about them?"

Miss Minerva got out her folder and began paging through it until she found the entry about the Feeding Grounds.

Fred could feel himself turning stubborn. He made up his mind he was going to see the grizzlies. If she didn't like it, she could kick him out of the car and he'd go it alone.

Miss Minerva read aloud. "The grizzlies are a larger bear than the black bear and quite easily dominate them. Some grizzlies weigh as much as 1,000 pounds, though most of the mountain grizzlies weight around 800 pounds. They are a bold animal and before the invention of the rifle they were indifferent to hunters. Except when goaded or cornered, the grizzly is a retiring creature, even shy. Except for the feeding grounds, he is, unlike the black and the cinnamon bear, rarely seen in the park." Miss Minerva read the last several sentences with some reluctance.

"See, there you go." Fred took a left into the feeding grounds. He pulled up in the parking area.

Miss Minerva looked at the shadows under the pines as if she expected a horde of grizzlies to rush out at them. "Please, let's get out of here."

Fred spotted a ranger standing off to one side. "I'll be back in a jiff." He got out of the car and went over to have a talk with the ranger.

"I'll drive off without you," Miss Minerva called after him.

"Go ahead. Just throw my suitcase on the ground."

The ranger was a veteran with deep crinkles around his eyes and gray fuzzy hair over his temples. His eyes were crystal clear blue and as hard as diamonds. "What can I do for you?"

"Well, my partner and I were wondering how dangerous it is to look at the grizzlies." Fred looked around the area. "Where are they, by the way?"

"In the woods. They usually don't come down out of the hills until evening when we feed them." The ranger pointed across toward a raised concrete feeding platform. "At that time tourists are permitted to sit in that enclosed seating area." The ranger next pointed to some wooden benches behind a woven wire fence.

"Oh, rats. And I so wanted to see one."

The Rolls-Royce pulled up beside Miss Minerva's Essex. Again all three, father, mother, daughter, got out of the car and wandered over toward where Fred and the ranger stood talking. This time the old gentleman flourishing a gold-tipped cane.

Fred liked the girl. He decided to break the ice. "The ranger just told me the grizzlies only come down in the evening when they feed them."

The ranger nodded. "At the end of the day the help over at the Canyon Hotel brings the garbage down here for the grizzlies to feed on."

"I see," the girl said.

The old gentleman wasn't paying any attention to either Fred or the ranger. "I say, isn't that your grizzly over there?" He pointed his cane. "In that clump of bush there?"

The ranger looked, and exclaimed, "For godsakes. That's most unusual. Some of the old boys have come down to feed on those juniper berries. That I've got to record." He got out a small notebook and began writing in it, once looking at his watch. "Rocky Mountain Juniper."

Fred couldn't make out how many there were. He

193

stepped toward the raised feeding platform for a closer look.

"Hey, I wouldn't do that if I were you," the ranger warned.

Fred was intent on having a look at the grizzlies. He also knew the blond English girl was watching and he couldn't resist showing off a little. He bounded lightly up on the feeding platform.

"Hey, you!" the ranger cried after him.

Fred slowed on the far side of the platform, but when he still couldn't get a good view of them, he hopped down onto the thick duff, almost soundlessly, and advanced slowly toward the junipers. He finally made out four sets of powerful shoulders, all silver-tipped. The silver hair rippled in the morning sun as the grizzlies reached into the junipers and nibbled at the berries. What thick luxurious hair. Back home Fred loved to lie on a bear rug Ma often spread on the living room floor. Winters he liked to nuzzle himself to sleep on it, taking his afternoon nap at the foot of the softly crackling hardcoal burner.

Behind him everybody fell silent.

Fred stepped quietly but determinedly around his side of the clump of junipers. There they were. Four of them all right. Old boys. And my God, were they great old fellows, coming almost to his chest as they stood on all fours. They weren't getting into each other's way, just quietly nipping at opal berries they found on their way through the clump.

Fred stood absolutely still. He made it a point to breathe evenly and slowly. He looked each grizzly over from snout to tail. They were as clean of crud as any of Pa's horses after a currying. Groomed by wind and water. Fred couldn't get over it that such hugely muscled creatures had such a delicate way of nibbling at

194

the opal berries. Not even Pa threading a twine string through a binder needle had been as finical.

Fred wondered what they saw in a juniper berry. He picked himself one from a nearby bush. Hmm. Bracing medicinal taste. It cleared the nasal passages. Had Ma known about them she probably would have made one of her herb teas from them.

The nearest grizzly slowly wryed his head around. The old boy looked at Fred with amused eyes, crooked his head once, lifted his snout and sucked a draft of air from around Fred toward him, then slowly swung his huge head back to his dainty nibbling.

Fred decided that was enough. He backed off slowly and then, making sure his oxfords made no cracking noise in the duff, turned and climbed up on the feeding platform.

He was privately congratulating himself that not once had he felt fear, that it was probably that lack of fear the grizzlies recognized and so had left him alone, when he was startled to see the blond English girl standing on the edge of the feeding platform and looking down at the grizzlies. She had watched him examine the grizzlies closeup.

The English girl smiled at him. "Bravo."

Fred gave her a little smile, shaking his head. "You shouldn't have come that close. Didn't you hear the ranger?"

"Yes, I heard him."

"Well then?"

"I felt so long as you thought it safe it would be safe for me."

Fred remembered his manners. "We haven't been introduced. Your parents won't object?"

"Whatever for? We're just doing America . . . sightseeing."

195

Fred was sure she almost said slumming. "Anyway, I'm Frederick Feikema." He turned up the edge of his red college sweater to let her see the lettering of his name. "And I suppose sightseeing is what I'm doing too."

A lovely smile opened her face. Her pink lips were full, rich, and her teeth perfect and very white. An extra light shone in her blue eyes, heightening the effect of the dark dot of her pupils. "Really." Then, "Your name is like that of a well-known English artist. Tadema."

"You through college?" Fred asked; and having asked, knew it was a dumb question. She'd probably gone to a finishing school.

"Well, yes, as a matter of fact I am. I had my last year at your Radcliffe."

"Really."

She held out her hand, flat, for him to take the fingertips. "And I am Geneva Hotham, from Wessex, England. And that's my father waiting over there, Sir Sedley Hotham, and my mother, Lady Georgiana Hotham." She pronounced Hotham as Huth'em.

Holy smokes. Fred instantly forgot the grizzlies. He could almost smell Thackeray in her. He thought of *Vanity Fair.*

Her warm smile continued. "Having gone to Radcliffe of course I recognized you as a college student."

"Otherwise you wouldn't have talked to me?"

She laughed. "I don't know."

Fred helped her down off the feeding platform and strolled slowly with her toward their cars. He liked it very much that she was tall, and slim, and that she had an elastic swing in her walk, almost undulating like a swimmer. He looked at her left hand, her ringfinger, and was glad to see she was wearing neither diamond ring nor wedding band. He wished he could prolong the walk.

Out of the corner of his eye Fred saw Miss Minerva frowning furiously. "Well, I see my old she-rip ain't very happy seeing me talk with you."

"She your mother?"

Fred almost burst out laughing. "No, thank God. No, my mother was more like you. This lady here, Miss Minerva Baxter, is a spinster from Chicago, and she's going to visit her brother in Boise, and she needed a driver and picked me up in South Dakota."

"That is different."

Fred caught what she meant.

The ranger stepped up. He was angry. "You know of course I could fine you."

Fred smiled. "It was at my own risk."

"But you might have got hurt and then it would have been my neck."

"Well, actually, I'm sort of a grizzly myself. Too big to get scared."

Miss Minerva beckoned Fred over with a finger. "We've got to hurry if we're going to make it to the Old Faithful before dark."

"Yes, Miss Minerva." Fred gave Miss Geneva a look to say he was sorry they had to break it off.

Lady Hotham wasn't too pleased either with what she'd seen. She had a frown almost as dark as Miss Minerva's. The old gentleman bent his head forward a little and stared at Fred with keen grey eyes. He thought Fred's daring act rather sporting.

The ranger wasn't quite done. "I think I ought to have your name, young man."

Miss Minerva grabbed Fred's arm. "Get in the car and let's be off." She almost dragged Fred along.

Fred said over his shoulder, "I'm sorry, sir. But really,

197

I wasn't afraid. I was raised around animals."

The ranger stared at Fred.

Fred got in on his side and Miss Minerva on her side and in a moment they were off.

The Yellowstone River on their right began to quicken and to curl a leaping white as the riverbed dropped.

Fred spotted a pair of swans flying low over the tumbling water. Trumpeter swans, if he'd read his folder right. Once paired, trumpeter swans were known to stick together for the rest of their lives. He watched them as he drove along. They were winging their way toward the canyon. Had Special Face only accepted him he would have been perfectly willing to fly down a canyon with her for the rest of his life.

He watched the swams drift along for almost a mile. They floated with the grace of professional figure skaters.

The road took a little turn and the next moment Fred heard some poetry in his head. He cocked his head to one side to listen:

> "There lay Yellowstone Lake
> black waves dancing blue
> washing up the sky.
> There walked the solemn moose,
> great-combed,
> dredging the tumbling streams.
> There flew the trumpeter swans
> paired in long white flight
> winging up the canyon."

He could see the flowing words as if written with acid on zinc. "I gotta remember to jot them down tonight when we stop."

"What?" Miss Minerva said.

"Nothing."

Next came the Upper Yellowstone Falls. Fred was of a mind to stop, but Miss Minerva, seeing his foot come up off the footfeed, waved him on. They really didn't have the time to stop for everything.

Fred watched the Rolls-Royce follow them in his rear view mirror. The Hothams didn't stop either. So it was all right.

They rolled past the Grand Canyon Lodge, an L-shaped building made of logs and wood shingles. A couple dozen cars glinted in the sun in the parking lot.

Immediately beyond it, Fred spotted a big sign pointing to the Lower Yellowstone Falls. Fred's eye picked out the figure *308 ft.* Holy suffering peter. That had to be some falls. And that he had to see. Without even a glance at Miss Minerva he pulled up in the scenic view parking area. Up in the rear view mirror he saw the Rolls-Royce turn in behind them.

Miss Minerva let go an old maid sigh. "Is this something we must see?"

Fred pointed. "It says a 308-foot drop of water here."

Miss Minerva almost blanched. "I can't stand heights."

"Oh come now, this is something you'll want to tell your brother about."

"No."

"Okay. Have it your way. I'll be back in a jiff." Fred got out. He spotted a footpath marked Uncle Tom's Trail and headed down it. Looking back over his shoulder, he saw the three Hothams lean over a railing and watch him go down. He tapdanced down some wooden steps, then the trail again, then some stone steps, finally hit an observation platform near the bottom of the canyon.

199

Looking up he saw it, a wall of water pushing off a great high cliff. As the great throw of water hit air it exploded into a cloud of falling drops. Then the falling drops disintegrated into a spreading swirl of spray, white at first and then gray. Near the bottom the burst flood disappeared into its own mist. Little erratic gusts of canyon wind carried some of the mist out to where Fred stood. The vapors swished past him and settled on the walls of the canyon behind him.

Fred found the breathing heavy, as much from the suffocating moist air as from the stupendous sight.

He stared until some movement above him caught his eye. It was Miss Geneva pointing toward where he'd parked the Essex. Yes. Miss Minerva was probably getting antsy again and calling for him. Reluctantly he left the observation platform and started back up.

The climb was a stiff one and he was puffing when he reached the top. He found the Hothams still busy staring off to the right at the falling white water. Sir Sedley had got out a cigarette holder and was smoking.

Out of habit Fred reached for his makings in his shirt pocket; paused when it hit him he hadn't smoked in a while. Truth to tell he really didn't feel the need to smoke that moment. The elevation in the park caused him to lose his taste for the weed, much like a bad cold often did.

Fred gave Miss Geneva a little wave of the hand to thank her for reminding him of Miss Minerva and hastened back to the Essex.

Fred was silent as he started up the motor.

He headed the car west, taking the road across the middle of the figure 8 loop.

Presently Miss Minerva asked peevishly, "Now, was that really worth stopping for?"

"Please, Miss Minerva, don't be such a crab."

200

"Well, I like that! When I'm giving you a ride."

"Look, if you don't want me to drive for you, just say so and I'll get out. Gladly."

Miss Minerva shut up. She looked darkly at the dashboard.

The crosscut turned out to be a freight road through heavy timber. It was rough and a driver was continually being warned that the speed limit, strictly enforced, was 25 miles an hour.

Looking up in his rear view mirror Fred was sorry to see that the Rolls-Royce wasn't following them. The English family had probably decided to see the upper part of the Grand Loop road.

Soon great columns of steam appeared above the evergreens ahead. That had to be the Norris Geyser Basin. Around another turn, and there was the Norris Ranger Station, a peeled-log building painted a dark brown. Immediately beyond it the freight road they were on rejoined the Grand Loop road coming down from the north.

"Do we want to stop for this geyser basin?" Fred asked.

Miss Minerva's eye caught something on a huge sign alongside the road. "Oh, I've heard of this place. It's where the Morning Glory Pool is. I want to see that."

"Good." Fred pulled up into a parking area.

Miss Minerva got out briskly. For once the view was free of tall peaks and deep canyons and she felt more at ease.

They strolled past various bubbling hot springs and boiling pools. Miss Minerva barely paused for Bathtub Spring, a trembling pool resembling a bathtub, or Emerald Spring, a muddy bubbling puddle. The smell around was gaseous. It reminded Fred of Ma's am-

201

monia bottle and window-washing time.

The Morning Glory Pool turned out to be a tiny thing, and not the famed one. Miss Minerva was disappointed and complained to a ranger about it.

The green ranger cocked his head to one side. "Sorry, Madam."

"But I consider that mislabeling."

"Sorry."

"Well, Frederick, let's move on then," Miss Minerva said.

Fred went back to the car with her.

The road was once again oiled. They headed slowly southwest. Fred wanted to stop at the Gibbon Cascades and Beryl Spring, but Miss Minerva vetoed it.

Honeycombed rock walls forced the road to run close to the Gibbon River. The deep green grass along the riverbanks was speckled thick with sunflowers and goldenrod. A wonderful smell of moist roots hung in the air.

Madison Junction came up, with the inevitable peeled log museum.

Fred pointed to a junction road winding off to the right. "Now when we come back here tomorrow from Old Faithful, that's where we'll go. It heads out some twelve miles to West Yellowstone, just across the border into Montana. The road splits there, and my road 187 goes north, and your road 191, goes south."

Miss Minerva's upper lip curled away from her teeth a little.

They rolled on. Fred thought the rushing and roaring black water under the burnt-over walls of the Firehole Canyon a sobering thing.

When the Fountain Paint Pot came up, Miss Minerva decided she also had to see that. They got out, brushed down their clothes, and took a winding trail through some trees.

Miss Minerva fell in love with all the different colored boiling muds, pink and calcimine and brown. "One can almost imagine the Good Lord dipping his brush in them when it comes time to paint the trees in the fall."

Fred didn't think much of the place. He thought it but a blubbering cauldron of hot mud.

When they got back to the car, Miss Minerva got out her grocery bags. "Time to have a snack."

Fred didn't object. His stomach had been growling for an hour. They sat with both car doors open to a soft sourish breeze coming off Firehole Lake, munching sandwiches and helping themselves to some fresh spring water. Fred noticed that the ink stains on Miss Minerva's fingers had finally disappeared.

Miss Minerva asked Fred for his map of the park and studied it for a while. At last she found reference to the real Morning Glory Pool. It was a mile up the road. "That's the one I want to see."

"The Opal Pool and the Turquoise Pool and the Sapphire Pool come first. Shouldn't we stop for them too?"

"No, I just want to see the true Morning Glory Pool, that's all."

When they finally pulled up in front of the Morning Glory Pool, they found a couple dozen other cars already glinting in the parking area.

Miss Minerva got out of the car all business. She was beginning to make a pilgrimage of the glory pool. She hated the park, but if she had to endure it because her driver wanted to see it, well, then she was going to find at least one thing she could enjoy.

Fred and Miss Minerva joined some twenty others standing beside the pool. One glance and Fred had to admit it was lovely. It did resemble an enormous morning glory, perfect in its sweeping irregular symmetry, with a white fringe and a morning blue color reaching all the way into its throat. Fred noted an interesting phenomena occurring in his eye — one moment the pool was a magnificent huge morning-glory flower, the next moment an interesting funnel-shaped hole in the earth filled with strange clear blue water.

Miss Minerva murmured beside him. "It's a wonder of the Lord's. Truly, here is proof that our Lord and Maker has been at work. That we should cleave unto Him for salvation."

Fred saw other nearby tourists look funny at her.

She placed a hand on Fred's elbow. "Don't you agree?"

"Well, back home we considered the morning glory a pest. It choked the corn. If you didn't root out that first morning glory, your whole field would soon be infested with them. And there'd be no crop of corn."

The tourists around the pool began to smile a little.

"Och!" she cried. "I'm not thinking of your cornfields. I'm thinking of the beautiful flower you grow in your garden."

"It's the same one. It's just that it's gone wild."

"You're always spoiling something for me."

"Lady, back home as a kid I had to pick, root out, those damned morning glories. Stooping all day in a hot sun. And if you didn't get all of the root, Pa made you go digging for it like a dog until you got it."

Miss Minerva didn't like the attention they were getting around the pool. "If you don't like it, go back to the car and wait. I mean to enjoy it." She looked at her wrist watch. "At least for fifteen minutes. Then after that, we'll go straight to the Old Faithful camping grounds to make sure we get a good safe cabin tonight."

Fred cocked an eye at her. "It's going to be a log cabin then tonight?"

"For both of us, yes."

"Now you're talking." Fred gave her a little bow, and retreated to the car.

While Fred waited, he got out his notebook and jotted down the lines of poetry he'd thought of earlier.

Fifteen minutes wasn't enough for Miss Minerva. Watching through the windshield Fred saw three different sets of tourists come and go while Miss Minerva continued to linger at the rim of the delicate volcanic phenomena.

Fred next got out his wordbook and studied a couple of pages of new words.

Pretty soon he saw her take something out of her purse and throw it in the middle of the glorious blue pool. For godsakes, an offering of some kind, he thought.

He heard a car come crunching up on the gravel beside the Essex. Mildly curious, he looked around. The Rolls-Royce. He was going to see the beautiful English girl Miss Geneva Hotham some more. She was sitting on his side and was smiling warmly at him. She too was glad that they had happened onto each other again. The driver got out and opened the rear door of the Rolls-Royce. One by one the Hothams got out, the two women brushing down their dresses, and the old gentleman checking his impeccable fly. For the first time Fred noticed their clothes. The two women were wearing gray dresses, very good for the dust and grime of travel. Fred had never seen gray material to beat it. It was subdued, of the very best cloth, and tautly conservative. The old gentleman also wore gray, worsted with a herringbone stripe.

Fred got out of his car too. "Well," he said, "to warm

205

over an old cliche, I see our paths cross again."

Miss Geneva's smile widened. The old gentleman twirled his gold-tipped cane once around a crooked finger. The old lady stared briefly at the sky. It was apparent that all three had had a discussion about that Amermican named Frederick Feikema.

Miss Geneva asked, "Is this worth seeing?"

Fred said, "Spoken like a true Miss Doubting Thomas from Radcliffe." He nodded toward Miss Minerva. "She's gone dotty over it. A little while ago I saw her throw in an offering, as if some god were hidden in it." He added, "But the Morning Glory Pool is very lovely. One look and you know why it's famous."

"Raally."

Fred wanted to make sure he'd see her again later in the day, so he said, "We're stopping at the Old Faithful tonight. I was wondering, you folks wouldn't be stopping there?"

"That was our plan."

"May I see you then? For a little while?"

Miss Geneva gave him an impish smile. "Will your lady friend give you permission?"

Fred snapped his hand down. "The hell with her. I'm not her slave."

"Hear hear."

Lady Hotham and the old gentleman had taken several steps up the path toward the Morning Glory Pool. "Are you coming with, Geneva?"

"In a moment, Mother."

Fred asked, "How long are you touring America?"

"Another month or so. We also want to see California and the Grand Canyon in Arizona."

"And then?"

"It's back to Merry England."

"And then?"

206

"Don't let's talk about that."

"Why not?"

"You really wouldn't want to know, would you?"

Fred reddened. He had been pushy. "I'm just kind of curious is all."

"And you? What will you be doing a month from now?"

"Don't let's talk about that," Fred said with a smile. "Actually though, I'll be looking for a job of some kind."

"What would you really like to do?"

"Travel. Write."

"Write? What kind of writing?"

Fred pawed the gravel path with the toe of his oxford. "Poems. Novels maybe."

"I see. How will you live?"

"That's the problem. Because I come from a farm family. And you know they've had a rough time of it the last few years. Besides, in our country, each generation is supposed to make it on its own."

Miss Geneva's blue eyes became a bit chilly. "Yass. And you said travel. How will you manage that?"

"I've got a friend who thinks he can get me a job on a boat. On the Dollar Line. I'll work my way across."

Miss Geneva made a little gesture with her hand for them to follow her father and mother. Miss Geneva thought to herself for a dozen steps, finally said, "Well, if you should ever happen to come to England, look us up. The Hotham castle, Wessex."

"Lady, if I ever do get across the pond, I surely shall."

Miss Minerva had once again spotted Fred talking with Miss Geneva and came hurrying up the path toward them. "Frederick. I've already spent far too much time here. We must get on if we're to make sure of good cabins for tonight."

Fred threw Miss Geneva a look. "See you later."

"At the Old Faithful."

"Yes."

After Fred had got the old Essex rolling again, Miss Minerva asked, "Those people aren't going to stop at the Old Faithful camp grounds now too, are they?"

"That's what Miss Geneva says."

Miss Minerva jerked erect on the seat beside him. Slowly she began to swell up. She began to look pretty black.

A half-dozen more signboards appeared along the way heralding interesting sights but Fred and Miss Minerva rolled on by. The ruggly gravel road continued to wind through a fabulous land.

At the Old Faithful camp grounds Miss Minerva spotted the office where cabins were for rent. "You stay here, Frederick. I'll be right back."

Fred had been having second thoughts about her doing him any more favors. "You don't need to rent one for me. I've decided I'm going to sleep under the trees. I've always wanted to do that out in the wild."

Miss Minerva looked into her purse once; then snapped it shut. "No, it's too dangerous. I'll get you a cabin." She stepped out of the car, then hurried off.

Fred thought: "You bet. What you mean is, you want to make sure I won't sneak out and have a rendezvous with that English gal Miss Hotham tonight." Sighing, he got out of the car too. He stretched himself, rising on his toes. Slowly he looked around. The Old Faithful Inn loomed up west of him, native logs, six stories high, steep gabled roofs. The Hothams would probably have dinner in it later on. Fred ran his fingers through his hair. "Somehow I've got to get in there while they're having dinner."

Fred knew there was no future in it for him with the

208

English girl. It wasn't so much she was out of his social class, because if it came to that, both his father and mother had some blooded family of their own in their backgrounds. It was more that Miss Geneva just plain had more money. Both of his grandfathers had an ardent love for the kind of freedom America offered. Social position, even royalty, could hardly match the American birthright of being born free. But sheer money could. It could even swamp a free spirit. Still and all, it would be fun to visit Miss Geneva in her castle.

Miss Minerva returned with a satisfied smile. "I've got us each a cabin. Now to buy us some groceries for our cookout, as you call it."

Fred held up a hand. "Wait. I think I'd rather have a light lunch in the Old Faithful Inn there. I'll buy. If you can get me a safe cabin, I can buy you a lunch."

"Lunch? But I'm famished."

"Well, then I'll buy you a dinner."

She hated to give in. She knew what he was up to.

"C'mon, lady. I know I'm eating at the Inn."

"Well . . . all right."

Fred helped her carry her suitcases into her cabin, then brought his own into his cabin. He was careful to hang onto his key.

A lean tanned ranger walking by asked if everything was all right.

"Fine," Fred said. Then Fred remembered something. "Say, when's the Old Faithful scheduled to go off next?"

The ranger looked at his watch. "In just about seven minutes. It isn't always exactly on time, you know, despite what the brochures may tell you. Generally the eruptions come about 65 minutes apart. But they've also been known to vary as much as thirty minutes."

"How come that?"

209

"It all depends on how much pressure has been built up each time down in those subterranean chambers."

Miss Minerva's face screwed up into a deep frown. "I don't think I care to see that."

"What!" Fred exclaimed. "When it's the greatest thing in the park."

Miss Minerva shook her head. "There's something about the idea of a spurting geyser that gives me the shivers."

"My dear lady, a geyser can't rape you."

The lean ranger threw a funny look from Fred to Miss Minerva and back to Fred again.

Fred laughed a little for the ranger's benefit. "I fear my traveling companion here is prone to see a man under every bed she sleeps in."

"Oh."

Miss Minerva continued to look black. "It smacks of the obscene. Something that only a man would enjoy."

Fred shot the ranger a look. "You see?"

Miss Minerva gave Fred an angry look. "Let me know when the Old Faithful's through spouting. Because I'm hungry."

"All right, Miss Minerva." Fred gave the ranger a nod, and then headed for the geyser east of the inn.

The geyser sat in a three-sided natural amphitheater with low pine-covered hills rising behind it. At the moment its gray cone, a hundred feet in diameter and a dozen feet high, like an Indian mound, lay still. A crowd had already gathered for the next eruption. They stood on the lee side of the wind. Almost every one had a camera ready.

Fred took up a position on a hummock behind the crowd. It would give him a good view at the same time that he could watch out for the Hothams.

After a while Fred had the uncomfortable feeling that

a set of eyes somewhere was watching him. Miss Minerva, of course. She was probably sitting in her cabin on
the edge of her bed staring out at him and watching to
see if the Hothams had shown up. What a witch. She
really was beginning to act as if she owned him. Like
some damned jealous wife. Lord, imagine being married to her and having to sleep with her at night. The
thought of joining flesh with her almost made him gag.

He spotted the Hothams making their way from a
parking lot on the other side of the inn. They were
hurrying to get a good seat. He watched where they sat
down. After several moments Miss Geneva began looking mildly through the crowd. She was looking for him.

The earth under them began to mumble. There was
a sound as if some earth monster had a frog in its throat
and was trying to clear it. The mumbling became a
deep rumbling. The sound of it was like the Great
Northern crossing the railroad trestle south of town
back home. Then steam rose out of the tube in the
center of the gray cone. Next came spilling hot water,
running down the sides of the cone like milk boiling
over. The hot water in the tube rose, became a bouncing column of steaming water. People all around Fred
began to oh and ah. The camera buffs clicked away,
one eye all screwed up. Fred thought them dumb asses.
People with cameras never really got a good look at
what was happening; only their camera did. Higher and
higher rose the column, whoozing and gruffing, until it
attained a height three windmills high, at least a
hundred feet or more. Click, click, click, went the
cameras. The murmur of the crowd became a loud
hum of appreciation. The great column of white drop-
dazzling water hung up there and hung up there. A
gentle breeze came along and opened out its top as
though a flag were being unfurled from a standard. The

loud hum of the viewers became almost a roar. Then in the vapor several fleeting rainbows appeared.

"What a show!" one woman cried.

"She sure came this time," a youth said.

"Ronald, you!" a girl sitting next to him said, giving him a reproving jab in the ribs.

Separate drops floated away from the column on all sides. The drops turned to fiery prisms in the sun. The gods were scattering aerial diamonds.

It was almost too big for poetry. What could a poet say about it and not feel foolish? The separate drops were perhaps worthy of being caught in poems, but the whole spectacular phenomenon? Too big. It would take a novel. An epic.

Slowly the column began to collapse. A phallus falling in on itself. Paling fallen veins. Down. Down. At last no more bubbling water could be seen. Only a few stray wisps rose from the tube. Meanwhile the water that had been discharged continued to flow down the ribbed sides of the gray mound, leaving strange traces of burnt brown and rusty orange and gravestone gray.

Fred remembered he'd better have some money ready for the little dinner he was going to have with Miss Minerva, so he took off his shoe and dug out the rest of his dollar bills, five of them. He placed them in his billfold, with the other bill.

Sorry the show was over with, he slowly got to his feet. Knowing Miss Minerva would be watching him, he decided not to seek out the Hothams just then. They'd be in the inn later on anyway and he could then strike up some more talk with the blond Geneva.

Fred knocked on Miss Minerva's door. "Still famished in there?"

"Coming." Miss Minerva had been waiting for him. She stepped out with a grim face. She'd made up her

212

mind about something.

The cafeteria was almost filled. Fred let Miss Minerva lead the way down the cafeteria line. Miss Minerva helped herself to potato salad, barbecued ribs, orange jello, and coffee. Fred decided to go lean and took only the barbecued ribs, a piece of pie, and coffee.

Miss Minerva selected a table in a far off corner. She was going to make sure Fred would be hard to spot.

Fred wondered where the Hothams were sitting. He began to feel tight in the belly. Between bites he pretended to be admiring the great tall fireplace and the huge homemade clock and the big beams in the lofty ceiling. He was aware that Miss Minerva was eating her food with jerky motions.

Finished, Fred sipped at his coffee. He looked out of the big windows toward Old Faithful. In a few minutes it would go off again.

Miss Minerva sipped at her coffee too. Her lips twisted as inwardly she worked at what she had to say.

A firm hand fell on Fred's shoulder. Wondering who it might be, surely not Miss Geneva, Fred turned.

It was a male waiter, a college student working in the park for the summer. The waiter leaned down. "A party across the hall would like to know if you two would care to join them for dessert." The waiter pointed. In a corner across the inn sat the Hothams. They were looking at them.

Miss Minerva looked too. "You mean the both of us?"

The waiter nodded.

Fred got to his feet. "Of course."

Miss Minerva snapped. "What! Well, as for me, emphatically not."

Fred said, "Well, your ladyship, I think I'll accept their invitation though."

Miss Minerva cried, "You are deserting me then, are you?"

"No. It's just that I'd like to visit with that girl a while. And her parents. They like me."

Miss Minerva gave him an outraged face. "I'm not going over there."

"Oh, come on, Miss Minerva Baxter. What are you afraid of, that the young girl will seduce me? Like you were once worried those cow gals might have back in Ten Sleep?"

Miss Minerva's face blackened over. She sat like a stubborn bulldog.

Fred heaved a disgusted sigh; then, thanking the young waiter, headed for the Hothams.

The Hothams made room for him across from Miss Geneva. Miss Geneva had a good smile for him. Her blue eyes twinkled with tiny lights of merriment. Light from a nearby tall window cast a soft amber radiance over her gold hair.

Sir Sedley said, "What about the lady?"

Fred said, "Oh . . . yes . . . She said she's sorry she won't be able to join us. She expressed her regrets."

Sir Sedley nodded. Then he called a girl waiter over. He said to Fred, "We were going to have ices for dessert. What would you like?"

Fred had already had a piece of pie. "An ice for me would be just fine."

Sir Hotham held up four fingers. "A vanilla ice for all of us."

The girl waiter left.

Sir Sedley watched the girl vanish into the kitchen. He houghed to himself. "I must say that the help here in Amerrica is tip-top."

Miss Geneva gave her father an indulgent laugh. "There's more to a waitress than her legs."

214

Sir Sedley reddened a little. He turned to Fred. "Don't you think so? Both the men and women waiters here appear to be special."

"That's because they're all college kids, working their way through school. At least that's what I read in one of the bulletins last night."

"Oh, so that's it. No wonder." Sir Sedley gave his daughter a sly look. "Well, daughter, I was after all attracted to their brains and not just their . . ." Sir Sedley turned to Fred "What is it you call them here in America?"

"Gams."

"Gams. Ho. Yes yes. Their gams."

Lady Georgiana, who had been staring up at the ceiling, now leveled her sights at her husband. "I wonder, Sedley, was it my brains or my gaams you were interested in when we first met."

Sir Sedley's upper lip wrinkled into a little smile. "With you it was the way you could beat me at darts."

"Father," Miss Geneva said.

"Funny thing is," Fred said, "the word gam was once in use in England, late in the eighteenth century."

"You don't say."

Fred felt the hairs on his spine rise. Something was happening behind him. He turned; and saw Miss Minerva advanced stoutly upon them. "Excuse me," Fred said to the Hothams, and quickly standing up got ready to handle whatever it was Miss Minerva was going to do.

Miss Minerva came at him already jawing away. " . . . awfully unfair of you after agreeing to drive me as far as you could go to get me to my brother's without accident, and after I've fed you and housed you, and given you Christian example —"

"Shut up!" Fred said, holding up a hand, more to her

215

mouth than to her. "I don't have to listen to all that guff. Nor do my friends. Now if you'll just —"

"— since you are prone to evil . . . what?"

"I said, shut up!" Fred then turned to the Hothams. They were staring at him. "I'm sorry. There's nothing I hate more than to make scenes. But it seems my benefactrix is bent on just that."

Miss Minerva caught a little smile hovering on Miss Geneva's lips. "And I don't need any of your patronizing airs either, you Britisher!"

Fred got mad inside. He had enough. He said to Miss Geneva. "I'm sorry but I'm going to have to break this off. And I apologize for my country." He grabbed Miss Minerva by the arm and very firmly marched her back to their table in the far corner. He sat her down in her chair. Then he snatched up their two bills; legged it over to the cashier; and paid for them both. It cost him three dollars and seventy-five cents.

Miss Minerva ran after him. "What are you going to do?"

"You and I are parting company. Right now. You didn't have to act so possessive. Who are you to think you can own me body and soul? Including my lips in case I decide to kiss a pretty girl? I'm getting out of here. You shamed me in front of those fine English people, people I was just nicely getting acquainted with, and who I might have visited in England someday. Damn you." Fred broke off and hurried out of the inn.

He went straight to his cabin. Thank God he'd had the foresight to hang on to his own key. He got out his suitcase. He was about to leave the key in the door when again Miss Minerva came running after him. Before she could say anything, he stuck the key in her hand. "Here you are. I don't think you'll have any trouble getting your money back for this cabin. Tourist traffic is still

216

heavy and I'm sure they'll be glad to have it back to rent. Good-bye." Suitcase in hand he started walking toward the Grand Loop Road.

She ran after him. Her stout legs pounded on the graveled walk. She sounded like a dash man. "Frederick! Frederick! Please don't leave me here all helpless."

Fred ignored her.

"Frederick, you're leaving me in the middle of all these mountains and I can't drive my car in them. You know what I almost did in the Big Horns."

Fred whirled around on her. "Listen to me good. You know the road back to Madison Junction. We just came down it. It was level most of the way, wasn't it? That you should be able to drive. And you remember how when we passed through Madison Junction I pointed out a road going west? You take that road. On the map I noticed it was pretty level all the way to West Yellowstone. From there on to Boise the road should be level too, because it runs right alongside the Union Pacific railroad and a railroad's gotta have level terrain. Now, let me go and good luck. You'll make it. Goodbye!" Again Fred resolutely turned away from her and headed for the highway.

She followed a few hesitating steps; finally stopped.

Fred didn't dare glance around for fear that if he saw her face he'd feel sorry for her and relent and once again be in her grip.

"Frederick. Oh, Frederick, good luck to you too. I'm going to miss you."

Fred hurried even more to get away from her.

217

IX

A new Ford coupe, green with black wheels, rolled down a side road toward Fred. The driver stopped at the corner beside Fred, looking first to the right and then to the left for traffic.

Fred stuck out his thumb for a ride.

The driver spotted the thumb, wrinkled his nose, and was about to shake head no when his eye fell on the big gold C on Fred's maroon sweater. Then he reached across and rolled down the window. "All right, hop in. But I'm in a hurry."

Fred got in quickly, throwing his suitcase on the shelf behind the seat.

"Where you headed?" the driver asked.

"West Yellowstone. And from there Belgrade near Bozeman."

"You're in luck. West Yellowstone is where I'm going. I've got to catch the Union Pacific mail train by six."

"You haul mail then."

"Right you are." The driver was about thirty, had balding gold hair, cheeks almost as grainy as orange peel, and the sloped shoulders of a scatback. The driver turned right, goosed his motor, and in a moment was hightailing it down the road. "I hope you got a good stomach because I'll be going like a bat out of hell all the way."

Fred looked back at the sun. "Aren't we going east?" West Yellowstone had to be behind them.

"Yeh, for a little ways I gotta go east to finish picking up the mail around the lower part of the loop. But I'll get you to West Yellowstone fast, never fear. Quicker'n any other way you could do it."

"It's all right."

They crossed the Continental Divide twice. The mail driver cut corners where he could. When he saw no one coming toward him in the left lane on a winding turn he took the left turn to straighten the turn. He leaned left to go right; right to go left.

Fred began to have mixed feelings about the new ride. First a pesky particular Miss Minerva Baxter; then a mad driver of a mailman. From a cold potato to a hot potato. Fred noted that sometimes they were going well over 70 miles an hour around really fearsome curves. He began to appreciate how Miss Minerva felt coming down the west side of the Big Horns. Fred asked, "Ever get pinched?"

"Not yit."

"If you did, it would be kinda funny."

"How so?"

"Be a case of the government pinching the government."

The mad mailman didn't smile. His eyes were all alert for the road weaving toward them.

Fred saw very little of the passing landscape. Sheer rock walls, heavy timber, a tiny lake dissected by the road they were on, a brief wavering view of a couple of mountain peaks that looked exactly like a certain cousin's bare breasts, and then an incredibly steep descent toward the vast blue Yellowstone Lake. The mailman hardly used the brakes.

When they hit the bottom of the valley they were at West Thumb. The mailman pulled up with a rush and a squealing of brakes in front of the ranger station. The Ford coupe almost rebounded from the setting of the handbrake, the motor still running, and the mailman was out with a leap and gone.

Fred felt like a smoke. He was about to fumble out his cigarette makings, when the ranger station door popped

220

open and the mailman came at him on the dead run carrying the mail pouch like a football. The pouch landed on top of Fred's suitcase. The mailman bounced in behind the wheel, slipped the Ford into gear soundlessly, goosed her, and was off, letting the momentum of the car slam the door shut for him.

They followed the shore of the deep blue dappling Yellowstone Lake going like the devil. The road quartered back and forth in a northeasterly direction. With the sun setting behind them the light kept bouncing off the blue water toward the east. The lake was so wide that only the higher mountains, Grizzly Peak and Avalanche Peak, poked out over the watery horizon.

The mailman pointed to a little island some distance from the shore. Two fishing boats were anchored near it. "Know what they're up to? That island is actually the dome of a boiling hot spring. Fishing Cone. When they catch a fish they just toss it over their shoulder into that boiling hot water and in a couple of minutes they've got themselves the freshest boiled fish anywhere in the world."

Fred threw him a disbelieving look.

"Fact."

Fred watched the fishermen narrowly. Fishing Cone looked a little like a teakettle almost submerged in water. Then the Ford coupe, going fast, took a turn in the road, and the fishermen and the boiling water island vanished from sight.

They zoomed up along the lake shore. Once they cut across a point. They had one narrow escape after another. Pretty soon they had so many narrow escapes Fred decided it couldn't be just luck; it had to because the mailman was just one helluva good driver.

Again at the Fishing Bridge post office the mailman pulled up with a squealing of brakes. Within seconds,

221

before Fred could get up a good laugh again about the wonderful time he'd had with Miss Minerva in that very place when she thought he was the hairy bear under her bed, the mailman rushed back and bounced in beside him, and with a deep goose of the motor was off.

Thought of Miss Minerva made him regret, for a few fleeting moments, that he'd been so rough with her at the end there. He could have bid her good-bye in a more gentlemanly fashion. As Sir Hotham might have done had he been in his place.

Thought of Sir Hotham brought back memory of the girl Geneva. It struck him again that Miss Geneva looked more like a girl of the twenties than the thirties. Aunt Gertrude, Pa's sister, had that look in the early twenties, especially that time when she took him to Hodge's Cafe in Doon for a sundae and they'd sat on strange wire chairs eating daintily from a glass-topped iron table. Miss Geneva had that same incredibly thin waist line and wasp-like belly.

They flashed by Dragon's Mouth. That was where he'd first met Miss Geneva. In reverie, daydreaming, he imagined a scene where, somehow, accidentally yet naturally, she'd slipped and fallen against him and he'd had to catch her, and then, as she looked up at him, smiling because now they had a little secret together, he leaned down and kissed her lightly, lips just barely sticking together a little like cigarette paper just licked. And she'd kissed back, equally light. And then —

"I damned near got killed here one time," the mailman broke in.

"Yeh?"

"Two queers. They were fighting like a couple of female cats in the front seat as they were backing out of the parking lot, and were so lost in the argument, they rolled across the road right in my path."

"God. What'd you do?"

"I made the guess they wouldn't see me in time, so I took the left lane, over on the shoulder as far as I dared to go, and made it."

"Close call."

"You should've seen their faces as I streaked by. I got a good look at them in the rear view mirror. I was afraid they'd roll over the edge of the road and drop down into the Yellowstone gorge there."

Fred shook his head to show he got the picture.

Again at Canyon Junction the mailman pulled up sharp; dashed in for the mail pouch; flashed out and jumped into the car on the run; and they were off, heading west down the crosscut freight road.

The mailman drove even faster on the nearly deserted road. Several times Fred saw the speedometer needle hover near 80. But Fred was getting used to it. He trusted the driver.

It was very strange to be flying down a road he'd taken earlier in slow motion in the old Super Six Essex. It was like a dream being redreamed, only faster. One more time around the lower half of the Grand Loup and he'd probably feel he'd just about lived there all his life.

At the Norris Geyser Basin they stopped for the usual pouch of mail.

At Madison Junction the same.

And then they headed down a new road. Fred sat up alert for fresh sights and smells. The sun was almost directly in their eyes. Sometimes it lay so low ahead it appeared to be part of the radiator cap, a fancy embellishment specially made by the Ford people. It was sometimes hard to see ahead, to make out the traffic coming as well as going. Luckily the road was almost straight. The road curved sharply in only one place,

223

around the base of Mount Jackson. They were following the Madison River, first on its left bank, then on its
right. Willow groves flashed by, then clumps of
chokecherries, then thick stands of pine. Occasionally
an open meadow exploded in front of them. Sometimes
below in the river driftwood lay piled up on great
boulders, almost choking it. The glowing river had a
wierd green color and through the open window Fred
caught the whiff of a mushy moss smell.

They passed through a thick stand of stiff straight
pines. The air darkened around them. The smell of
pine knots made a fellow dizzy, as if he'd been
breathing too fast for too long.

"There she is," the mailman said casually. "We
made it."

Fred thought he meant the few buildings lying ahead
in a little valley. There was a log store-and-cafe, a log
depot, and an almost windowless building also made of
logs. "So that's West Yellowstone."

"I meant that train waiting there."

"Oh." Through a picket-like row of trees Fred spotted the engine. White steam was pulsing out its tall
black stack. Its petcocks were hissing flying vapors.

The mailman pulled up in front of the depot. He
looked at his watch. "Right on the dot." He reached for
the several mail pouches and stepped out. "Well, this is
as far as I go."

"Thanks a lot for the ride." Fred smiled wryly. "It
was a little faster than I planned on seeing the rest of the
Yellowstone National Park, but by golly, I can now
claim I know what it's going to look like in a fast reel
movie."

"Ha." With a quick liquid shrug the mailman tossed
the mail pouches over his shoulder, and was gone.

Fred picked up his suitcase and stepped out. He stood

looking uncertainly up and down the short street. Besides the three downtown buildings, he made out a half-dozen houses set back in the trees. There was no hotel or tourist cabins. He looked west down the road and saw where 187 split off from 191 and went north. 187 was the route he'd have to take. And the other route Miss Minerva would take. He was satisfied, after the ride with the mailman, that she'd be able to make it. The road had been fairly level as he'd told her.

Two cars stood outside the store-cafe. One of them, an old touring model Ford, had a star painted on it. Sheriff's car.

The sheriff's car gave him an idea. He'd gone far enough for that day. It was time to think about where he was going to sleep that night. He trudged over to the store-cafe. Inside there were only two people, the proprietor behind the counter and a slim older man sitting on a stool having a cup of coffee.

The proprietor was a short dark fellow who looked like he might have some Indian blood in him. He looked at Fred's height with interest. "You play basketball?"

"Did."

"Center?"

"Yep." Fred settled on a stool at the end of the counter.

"College?"

"Yes."

"Too bad. Man, could we have used you a couple of years ago on our high school team. We had two hotshooting forwards, one guard who was a tiger on defense, another guard with a hardnose to bring the ball down and who could hit from outside. But we needed a center to rebound for us."

"Where was this?"

225

"Bozeman High School."

"I didn't play basketball in high school."

"You din't?"

"No. I had to work my way through. And I didn't start to grow until my senior year."

"Work your way through. Now that I like to hear. Not, hey, Ed?"

Ed was the skinny man sipping coffee. He'd been pretty much minding his own business, though his ears had been working. Skinny Ed nodded.

The proprietor smiled large white teeth. "Well, what'll you have?"

"Hamburger." Fred pointed at a glass container. "And a piece of that blueberry pie there."

"Burger up."

Fred waited until he was about finished with his blue pie. "I noticed a sheriff's car standing out there. Is he around?"

The proprietor pointed a glowing cigarette at the skinny man. "That's him."

"Well." Fred turned to Ed with interest. "I would never have taken you for a sheriff."

"You wouldn't, huh?"

"No. You're not wearing the typical uniform we see in the movies. And you're not wearing a gun."

Ed smiled.

The proprietor said, "Ed don't believe in guns." He turned to Ed. "I don't think you've ever worn a gun, have you? Even that time when you had to go into the bush and bring out that Sheepeater Indian you didn't wear one."

Ed smiled some more. "If I can't talk 'em out of the bush, they's no use of bringing 'em in. Might just as well leave 'em out there if they're self-supporting. I don't believe much in jails anyway."

Fred liked what he heard. One night he'd argued long and valiantly with fellow members of the Plato Club at Calvin College that the state did not have the right to take a life for a life, that furthermore jails did not work to improve the prisoner but instead made him worse as it threw him in with revenge-bent convicts.

Ed pushed his cup toward the proprietor. "How about another lick of that black poison."

"Coming up."

Ed sugared and creamed his coffee, then turned to Fred. "What do you want with the sheriff?"

"Well, I tell you. I'm hitchhiking to a friend of mine up north in Belgrade, and I've only got a couple of bucks left, and I thought I could save some money if I could get a bunk in a local jail."

"Oh."

"I noticed when I hit town here there was no hotel or tourist cabins. And I first thought I'd sleep out under the pines, on the soft duff, but after the scare a park ranger threw into me for daring to walk up close to some grizzlies, I don't think I better try that."

"No, you shouldn't." Ed sipped his black poison. "Have you done anything wrong so I can use that as an excuse to throw you in?"

"Not that I know of. Unless hitchhiking is a crime."

Ed mused to himself for a while. "Well, there is some kind of dumb law about migrants. Vagrancy." He looked at Fred's sweater. His lightgrey eyes sharpened when they fell on the label on which Fred's name had been sewn. "That your handle?"

Fred held the label out for Sheriff Ed to see it better. "Frederick Feikema."

Ed mused to himself some more. "Well," he drawled, "you don't look buggy to me so I guess I can put you up. I don't wants bugs in my jail. This is still a clean coun-

227

try and I mean to keep it that way." He waved a slim hand at Fred. "When you finish up here I'll take you to your room"

Fred said, "I still have my coffee. Mind if I smoke?"

"No. You can smoke in here but outside we don't like it. We ain't never had a forest fire through here and we don't want you to start the first one."

Fred already had his makings out, but after that last remark by the sheriff, he put them back in his shirt pocket.

"Go ahead smoke."

"No, that hungry I ain't for the weed." Fred turned to the proprietor. "What do I owe you?"

"Two-bits."

Fred paid up. He had just two dollars left.

When they'd both finished their coffee, the sheriff stood up and crooked a finger at Fred. "Okay, Stretch, let's go."

The sun had just set and already darkness like a heavy purple damp had descended upon the little place. All the houses had lights on. Sheriff Ed went up the street to the almost windowless log building. He got out a ring of keys and selecting one opened the front door. He snapped on an overhead electric light bulb. Sharp light flooded over an old oak rolltop desk, a swivel chair, a green filing cabinet, and a web-spring cot. Beyond the cot was an iron grating and behind that several jail cells each with a similar web-spring cot. There was a smell of old mattresses in the place.

Sheriff Ed pointed at the cot in the office part. "That long enough?"

"I'm used to sleeping with my feet hanging over the end."

"Just for fun, try it once."

Fred set down his suitcase and draped his long frame

228

over the cot. The cot was far too short. The end of it cut Fred across the calves.

Sheriff Ed didn't laugh. "Hmm."

"No no. It's all right. I can sleep on my side, doubled up." Fred sat up. "And if I feel I have to lay stretched out for a while, well, I can sleep on the floor."

"I don't have a carpet. Just this log floor."

"When you're young you don't need a carpet."

"You're the doctor." Sheriff Ed's lightblue eyes glinted with amusement. "Now, Stretch, I'm gonna have to lock you in, you know. Them's the rules."

"That's all right."

"You won't get stir fever on me, will you? And start hollering in the middle of the night to be let out?"

"Not the way my brain is about to conk out after all I went through today." Fred told a little about Miss Minerva Baxter. He suggested that sheriff keep an eye out for her in case she got into trouble with her robot driving.

"Okay. And I'll watch out for her."

"I'd appreciate it a lot."

Sheriff Ed started to back out of the door. "Goodnight." A moment later his key clicked in the lock.

Fred studied the short cot, and then got an idea. His suitcase was almost as high as the cot. He set it at the front end of the cot, put out the light, and once again stretched out. That was better. The suitcase made it almost long enough. He kicked off his oxfords, letting them fall to the floor, and loosened his tie and unbuttoned his shirt collar.

He had just time to smile once more about the night before when Miss Minerva mistook Black Bimbo the bear for him, and to wonder about her notion as to what a naked man really felt like, when his brain began to whisper with sleep.

229

X

Fred awoke with the sun shining in the east window of the jail office. There was a wind out and the pines were whispering and jostling overhead.

The backs of his heels hurt where they'd hung caught over the edge of his suitcase most of the night. He felt a stretch coming in his toes and he let it undulate up the length of his body.

There were steps outside and then the light tickle of a key in the door, and then Sheriff Ed stepped in.

Sheriff Ed looked down at him with a private little smile. "How's my voluntary jailbird this morning?"

"Ready for breakfast and work."

"Hey, pretty good. Never heard that one before. Sleep well?"

"Wonderful." Fred swung his legs out of bed and sat up. He pulled on his oxfords and laced them. "Teeth taste furry though."

"They always do after that black poison we had last night."

Fred stood up and snugged up his tie. "But I guess I better go back for another cup of it."

Sheriff Ed led the way outside and locked up. Then Sheriff Ed took Fred lightly by the elbow and turned him up a winding path leading through the pines behind the jail.

"What's up, Sheriff?"

"You'll see in a minute, Stretch."

Fred followed the sheriff up the path. Mountain jays challenged the right of way. Myriads of little birds chittered high in the creaking pines. The smell outdoors was wonderful: seeping rosin, crushed pine needles, blue air of the high altitudes. Sheriff Ed had a sly smile on his thin lips. Fred wondered what in God's name

231

was up.

Fred recalled part of the talk of the night before in the cafe. "That Sheepeater Indian you talked about, what kind of an Indian is that?"

Sheriff Ed waggled his lean head. "Don't know much about 'em." He had on a wide mountain hat that morning and its brim moved like wings. "A prof was down from the university one time and he said they was a people who lived up in the high parts of what is now Yellowstone National Park, long before even the Indian came. Said they was a non-Indian race of short people, mostly pygmy. If you ask the Sheepeaters themselves, they say their ancestors've always been here. 'From the beginning.' "

Fred nodded. The strangeness and the vastness of the country had already been overwhelming, but to learn that it also had an old history, well, that really made it jump in one's imagination.

Sheriff Ed turned off the path and headed for the door of a one-story log cabin. The log cabin was well-hidden from the other half-dozen houses. Smoke breathed up from its chimney. Sheriff Ed pushed the door open and called in, "Here's your boy, Mattie."

A well setup brown-haired woman turned from her work at the kitchen stove. She had a pancake turner in her hand. Her warm blue eyes surveyed Fred with wondering interest. She liked his height. "Hello."

Pancakes! Fred stared at several cakes frying on a griddle on the stove. "Hello." Then he shot a look at a log table near her. Already quite a stack of pancakes had been set out. Fred turned to the sheriff. "You mean, you've invited me to have pancakes with you?"

Sheriff Ed smiled. "You did say you was ready for breakfast and work, didn't you?"

"You bet."

232

The missus waved him to a chair. "Set to and help yourself."

Sheriff Ed interposed. "I think he wants to wash up first." He pointed to a sink and a small handpump. "Why don't you?"

Fred washed himself with good soap. He combed his hair in the mirror. He resnugged up his tie dead-center in his collar. "Okay, where do you want me to sit."

The missus pointed to a chair across from Sheriff Ed.

The pancakes were a wonder, as thick as a slice of bread and as light as angel food cake. Fred smeared on the butter until the brown cakes ran gold. Then he poured on thick dark flapjack syrup. It was all so fluffy sweet he could cut it with the side of his fork.

Sheriff Ed smiled quietly as he watched Fred gorge himself. And the missus began to cluck in pride over his gargantuan hunger.

Fred ate until he began to feel thick and sticky under his eyes. After the tenth pancake he had to loosen his belt one notch.

Sheriff Ed laughed. "Stretch, if you eat any more, you're gonna set a record for West Yellowstone."

"What is the record here?" Fred asked, managing to speak around a particularly succulent syrup-and-butter soaked bite of pancake.

"I think it was ten, wasn't it, Mattie?"

Mattie had a tear in the corner of her blue eyes. "He means our boy," she said to Fred. "Ned so loved pancakes."

"What happened to him?"

Mattie cried a little, and shook her head, and turned back to her griddle.

Sheriff Ed said soberly, "He went out one morning to climb Kock Peak up north of here and we never heard from him again. He and a buddy of his."

233

Fred's cheeks chilled over. He understood then why Sheriff Ed and wife Mattie had invited him in for a pancake breakfast. In delicacy, not wanting to break Ned's record, Fred stopped eating, "Search parties couldn't find him?"

"No." Sheriff Ed coughed. "Local gossip has it that the Sheepeaters got him. But of course I don't believe that. If there are Sheepeaters up there, they're peaceful. Otherwise they wouldn't stay out of our sight so. That is, if they really are up there."

"When they say Sheepeater, do they mean they steal your pasture sheep?"

"They catch wild mountain sheep."

"Oho."

"That's the best eating in the world."

"I never had any."

Mattie dropped two pancakes in her husband's plate and four in Fred's plate.

"I'm getting pretty full," Fred said, rubbing his stomach in a circular manner.

"Naw, eat up," Mattie said. "I've got batter for six more."

"What about yourself?"

"I never eat pancakes," Mattie said.

"Well . . ." And Fred, then not worrying any more about their son Ned's record, and still feeling hungry despite a distended stomach, pitched in for eight more. A total of eighteen. "This should last me until tomorrow morning."

Sheriff Ed laughed. "That many would last me a week."

Fred helped himself to some coffee. It tasted like Pa's coffee, strong and mellow both. Fred got out his cigarette makings. His mouth finally felt ready for a smoke. "May I?"

234

"Help yourself," Sheriff Ed said. "In here it's okay."
Mattie set out an ashtray for him.

The smoke tasted good all the way through. As Fred pinched out his cigarette in the ashtray, he regretted, as he often did, that breakfast was over and it was time to face life again.

Sheriff Ed said, "Where'd you say you were headed for again?"

"Belgrade. Up near Bozeman."

"Hmm. Tell you what I'll do. I have to go up to Jeffers today. I can take you up to the junction, where a spur going west cuts off from 187. That'll be a good place to catch a ride."

Fred thanked Mattie, and then quick said good-bye when he saw her face begin to break up.

Sheriff Ed had little to say as they pounded north in his old touring model Ford. The motor stunk of heated clean oil. They rode up a shadowed aisle, between high thick stands of lodgepole pine. Each shaft of tree was a mast furled out with green topsoil. They rode in shadow redolent with rosin and moss.

When they hit the junction, Sheriff Ed took the turn left and stopped. "This is as far as I can help you out, Stretch."

Fred stepped down with his suitcase. "Thanks for the great breakfast. And the lift too, of course."

"Don't mention it. Good luck now, son."

"Thanks."

The old Ford ground on. The sound of its hot motor died away like the slowly weakening purr of a cat.

Fred took up a spot beyond the junction so that he could catch cars coming in from the west as well as up from the south. The junction was in a clearing. The forest on all sides was set back a ways and up a series of rises. The sun shone on the black tar road. A dry creek

235

curled down from the north and passed under a culvert.

Fred wound his wristwatch and waited. Nine o'clock became ten o'clock. As the sun rose higher and higher most of the birds fell silent. Only the magpie and the mountain jays remained to scratch out food. As the air warmed the aroma of running rosin became stronger.

There was also another smell and for a long time Fred couldn't identify it. It reminded him vaguely of flowering milkweeds, except that it was more subtle. There was also the bouquet of honey in it. Honey. That was it. Somewhere in the woods there had to be a hollow tree full of wild bee honey.

Silence became a great noise. There was utterly no wind out yet the pines hummed, occasionally even broke out with overquavers, very high trilling. Every time he breathed the pine-drenched air a new tune started up in his head. The impulse to break out into song kept bubbling up in his throat. The music of silence, for all its delicate subtletry, boomed in his skull. There were times when he thought he'd burst with it all.

Eleven o'clock became twelve o'clock became one o'clock.

Fred got out his three favorite books and sat down to read a while, each in turn. Dipping into Shakespeare's *A Midsummer Night's Dream* while sitting in the middle of mountain forest was like reading it with a full orchestra in the background. Savoring Whitman's *Out of the Cradle Endlessly Rocking* was like crying over another man's nostalgia. And reading about Job and his boils in the Bible was like finding an even finer edge to what it meant to be alone and solitary.

The sun hit directly down at the black tar, bouncing off shafts of glinting irridescence, which, mingling with rising heat waves, made Fred think he'd been transported into the dream world of Camelot. For the

236

moment it would not have surprised him if a knight all pricked out with spear and horse ears had come riding down out of the mountains.

A black bear emerged from the forest across the road. For a few seconds Fred was sure it was coming directly for him. But it paid him no mind, not even snuffing or glancing his way, heading instead for an old fallen fat pine. Fred hadn't noticed the fallen pine before. The black bear twice lifted his nose and sniffed ahead toward the fallen pine. Then it hit Fred what the black bear was smelling. Honey. The black bear cautiously circled the fallen pine, wary of bees, then suddenly attacked it, smashing its half-rotted hull open with two solids whacks of its big forepaw. Instantly a little brown cloud of bees emerged. They swarmed over the black bear. But the black bear, wiggling its stub ears, ignored them and plunged in and began gulping big sliding hunks of dark honey. The black bear ate until he had his fill, then wiggling his tiny stump of a tail, galloped up into the pines to the north. The bees were so mad that a few even came out to where Fred stood and buzzed him. Fred stood absolutely still and presently they left him.

Two o'clock came along and still no cars. Then three. Then four.

About four-thirty Fred thought he heard a laboring motor coming up from the south. He watched the curve in the road, and sure enough presently a two-door Chevrolet coupe appeared. It was towing another car, an old touring car Chevy with its top down. As the two cars approached, Fred could make out three people in the first Chevy and two people in the back Chevy. The back seat of the second Chevy was packed full of camping equipment. Soon Fred also made out that the radiator of the first Chevy was boiling over. A continuous jet

237

of steam, like an inverted geyser, showed beneath its bumper, hissing down at the tar road.

The three people in the first car, a young man and two young women, spotted Fred. The young man driving appeared to want to stop, but the young woman next to him kept shaking her head. The other young woman said nothing. She was pretty and looked at Fred with interest.

The first Chevy took matters in its own hands. Its motor quit. It chugged to a stop right beside Fred.

The young man pulled up on the brake and slowly got out. He went around in front and opened the hood. Heat waves burst upward from the hot motor. With ginger fingers he slowly turned the radiator cap until, still turning, the radiator cap shot upward even as he jerked his hand back. There was a big gush of steam. The steam jetting downward under the motor stopped.

"Got pretty hot there," Fred offered. Fred saw that they hardly had room to give him a ride.

"Yeh," the young man said. He had a rueful red face and long eyes. He didn't look at Fred so much directly as he did peripherally. "That slowly rising grade finally got her." He looked at the dry creek bed. "Yeh, and there's no water there either. Shucks."

The young woman sitting in the middle of the couple wouldn't look at Fred. But the other young woman got out of the car. She said, "We got that Thermos jug of drinking water in the other Chevy, Bud."

"Yeh, I suppose we have at that." Bud set the radiator cap on the fender. The steam rising from the radiator slowly subsided to a vague vapor. It mingled with the heat waves rising off the hot motor. "But we're gonna have to set here a while to let her cool off first."

The young woman still in the car said, "Milly, get back in here."

"But why," Milly said.

"I don't like it."

"I don't get you, Cynthia."

Cynthia looked Fred up and down. Fred's height bothered her. Cynthia had the same look in her eyes that Special Face's mother once had for him back in Grand Rapids, that he might hurt Special Face.

Milly gave Fred a good country smile. "Have you waited here long?"

"Since early this morning."

"That long."

"I've about given up hope I'll catch a ride anymore before dark. Probably have to sleep out tonight."

Milly folded her slim freckled arms across her waist. She had the shape of a swift runner, slim curving calves, long slender waist, modest bosom, and long slender arms. Her bobbed brown hair was touched with a wine red and her eyes were as blue as the sky behind her. Her lips were like the slender inner petals of a peony. At last she turned to Bud, "You don't suppose we could give him a lift?"

Bud raised his shoulders. "We're overloaded already."

Fred said to Milly, "Thanks, but I might be just the straw that breaks the camel's back."

Milly fell into more thought. She thrust her hands into the pockets of her denim skirt.

The man in the open touring car stirred. "Ain't she about cooled off by now?" The man was old and a little beaten down by life.

"Couple of more minutes, Dad."

The woman in the touring car managed a wan smile. She too was old. "At least this is a relief from all that bumping."

The old man nodded. "You said it."

239

Cynthia continued to look away from Fred. Fred wondered what was eating her.

Bud went around kicking rubber, all eight tires. Then he went back to the radiator and peered in. "Seems to be cooled off enough now." He went over and fetched the water jug. "I'll start her up and Milly you pour the water in real slow now. Or we'll crack the block."

Bud got in and pushed the starter button. Surprisingly the coupe motor fired right off. Milly picked up the jug and started to pour water into the radiator. The radiator was high for her and she couldn't quite get a good angle at it. She spilled some over the side.

"Watch it," Bud called out. "We need every drop of that."

Fred stepped up. "Here, give it to me. I can do it easy. I'm just a mite taller."

Milly gladly surrendered the jug and Fred, hand steady, poured the water in easily, hitting the steaming rusty hole dead center. As he poured, he asked, "What's wrong with the back car that you gotta tow it?"

"Bearing out," Bud said shortly.

Water began to show in the hole and Fred quit pouring. He corked the jug and then screwed on the radiator cap.

Milly carried the jug back to the second car. Milly said something to the older woman in the second car, and the older woman, smiling to herself, nodded.

Cynthia leaned out of the coupe. "Milly, hurry up before the motor gets hot again."

Milly came back slowly. She looked at Fred. Then she turned to Bud, "Can't we put him up on the turtle? A little more weight isn't going to hurt that much, is it?"

Bud looked down at his steering wheel and let his lip push out. He threw a sidelong glance at Cynthia.

240

"Milly! Get in," Cynthia said.

Milly looked at where the sun was sinking. "In another hour the valley will turn cool and then the motor won't heat up so."

"That's true," Bud said.

Milly made up her mind. "Think you can hang on back there on the turtle?" Smiling, she pointed to the sloping trunk of the coupe.

Fred said, "I can try. Because I sure am getting tired of standing here."

"Hop to it," Milly said. She watched Fred swing his suitcase on the trunk, or turtle as she called it, and then settle himself sideways on it, feet hanging over the fender. "You sure you won't fall off?"

"No."

"Maybe you better sit facing the second car. That way you can brace your legs on the bumper."

"Good idea." Fred swung his feet around and hooked his heels in the bumper.

Sure that he was secure Milly got in. And in a moment, with a groan of the clutch, motor laboring and growling, the two-car caravan took off.

Slowly Bud built up speed. He knew how to nurse a motor and get the most out of it. It was a slow climb all the way. Even in the dips the motor labored. The slow vast tossing horizons threw off one's sense of what was level. The problem of what was level reminded Fred of Einstein's theory of relativity. The long shadows struck off by the sinking sun also helped to fool one.

The birds of the forest awakened, singing their evening ludes of love.

The sun hit the high tree line and then, when the two cars steadied in a dip, it disappeared. Instantly a cold wind came down out of the trees. Almost at the same time the motor began to run smoother and with more power.

They climbed. Fred guessed they were making about twenty miles an hour.

They topped a rise and started down. For a brief fleeting moment the tip of the sun, pink, once again glowed over the far green horizon, and then was gone for good. The two cars began to pick up speed, thirty miles an hour, forty miles an hour. The car behind, with the most weight, coasting, sometimes caught up with the front car and the chain between them hung slack, rattling on the tar road.

It became very cold up on the turtle and Fred had to huddle down and stick his hands under his sweater. And the wind tugged at him and he was hard put to it to keep his heels hooked on the bumper. He was afraid that if they ever hit a chuckhole he'd get bounced off and be run over by the second car. Fred began to practice in his mind what to do should he fall off. Try to dodge off to the right, and make a little leap for it, and then try to hit the earth rolled up in a ball.

Milly inside became concerned too. She began to look at him more often through the back window. She gave him a smile, secret from Cynthia.

It hit Fred that Milly and Cynthia were sisters, that Cynthia was married to Bud, and both women were daughters of the old couple in back.

Thank God the tar road was as smooth as a threshing belt. Off on the right hung Gray Peak and off on the left Koch Peak. Sometimes the forest on both sides came right down to the ditch of the road; sometimes it opened out into lovely clearings. Presently a creek showed up alongside the road, trickling with swift water, splashing over rocks, twisting, then shooting down the valley with the road. Very quickly it became a good wide stream, foaming as it cascaded over a series of drops. A sign

242

pointed toward the stream:

Gallatin River.

Fred recalled from the map that the river flowed all the way up past Belgrade. He was on the home stretch.

The cold worked on him. He had to flex his thighs, first one, then the other, to keep the cramps out. If he got a charlie horse up on that turtle he was done.

Milly saw him rubbing his thighs. She caught on and promptly began telling Cynthia and Bud about it. Cynthia refused to look and Bud was too cowed to look. Milly kept talking and pointing. Finally, when Bud still didn't do something, she became angry. Her eyes squared and her face turned pink.

Still Bud did nothing. He turned on the lights for something to do.

They hit a little rib in the road. At just that moment Fred was massaging his right thigh and had only one heel hooked in the bumper. He teetered up on one ham, hung precariously, almost tipped off, scratched with his fingernails at the edge of the trunk lid, finally caught one nail under the edge, and hung on. In a moment he got his balance, settled back, and got both heels hooked under the bumper again. When he turned his head to reassure Milly that he was all right, he found both women, Cynthia as well as Milly, staring at him in shock. A second more and then Cynthia said something sharply to Bud. Bud slowly applied the brakes. The two cars came to rest on a little cement bridge. The bridge spanned a tumbling stream coming down from the west.

Milly stepped out. "You better come inside with us."

Fred swung himself down and then his suitcase. "You think we can all get in there?"

243

Milly studied his suitcase. "I think we better put that in the back car." She picked it up as if she were used to swinging bales of hay. She lashed it down with the rest of the camp gear. She came skipping back. "All right. Get in first and then I'll sit on your lap."

Fred cleared his throat. With a delicate lick of his lips, he said, "Perhaps I should introduce myself. I'm Frederick Feikema. From Doon, Iowa."

"Hi. And I'm Mildred Meade. And this is my sister Cynthia. She's married to Bud. Bud Miller. And those are my folks in the back car. Pa and Ma Meade."

Fred nodded. He'd guessed right.

"Well?"

Fred settled into the car, leaving his right leg dangling out. Milly in turn swung in between his legs and settled on his lap. Fred then drew his right leg in and Milly closed the door after them with a snap.

Bud eased the car in gear and they were off.

Fred was still cold and shivered several times. Milly felt him and settled herself warmly on him. She glanced around and down at him and smiled. Fred could feel Cynthia sitting stiff beside him. He could feel it where her thigh, willy-nilly, had to touch his. It was a tight fit for three on the seat, and with Milly squashing him down all the more so.

The valley deepened, the Gallatin River widened, the mountains rose higher on both sides, and darkness swallowed up everything, until it appeared they were driving down into a long vast cave.

Milly moved on his lap. She was a warm burden. "I see by your sweater you went to college."

"Just graduated." Fred was grateful that Milly was willing to talk. It would help ease matters in the coupe. "Calvin College in Michigan." He lifted her up a little so her tailbone wouldn't quite dig so into his chilled

244

thigh. "How about you?"

"Just graduated too. From Montana State in Bozeman."

Fred liked that. In at least one respect they were kin.

Bud said, "I bet you played center in basketball."

"Yes, I did."

Bud nodded. "I played guard in high school. Didn't go to college."

Fred turned to Cynthia. "You go to college?"

Cynthia said, somewhat curtly, "No. And for all the good it's done Milly, I don't think it would have been worthwhile for me either."

Fred and Milly fell silent.

The road was deserted. No cars coming or going. The headlights of the Chevy coupe were sharp and lit up peripherally both sides of the road. Once they almost ran down what looked like a porcupine. It became warm in the coupe and after a while Milly opened the window a crack on their side. Instantly the acrid aroma of rosin, like the taste of horehound candy, entered the car.

Fred asked, "Were you people out camping?"

Milly said, "Not really. Every summer our family goes up in the mountains to herd sheep. So our camping out is really work, not pleasure."

"What did you do with the sheep?"

"We sold them all except for some young ewes. The young ewes are coming down by truck. We winter them back home on our ranch."

"Ah, you people own a ranch. That sounds wonderful."

Cynthia said, "It's a small ranch."

Fred gave Cynthia a smile to help her get used to him.

Cynthia said, "What are going to be? In life?"

"I haven't made up my mind yet," Fred said. "I could teach because I got a Teacher's Life Certificate

245

from the state of Michigan. But I want to look around first. Do a little traveling. Because once you settle down you won't do much traveling after that, what with a job, wife, and children."

"That's what I think too," Milly said, giving herself a little bounce and resettling herself on Fred's lap.

Cynthia didn't like Milly's bounce on Fred's lap and again her thigh tightened against Fred's leg.

Milly making herself at home on his lap gradually awakened Fred. He was sure she must be feeling a lump developing under her seat. It wasn't at all that she was flirtatious; just that she was an easy-does-it ranchland Western girl. Fred liked her. Though he didn't think he could fall in love with her. She didn't have that magic for him that Special Face had. Milly could become a wonderful friend, even a lover, but hardly his romantic love. She didn't quite have that shining outline, yes, that special face.

Milly began to talk about their ranch, and Cynthia kept asking her if she was going to take that job teaching in the nearby country school, the one they'd both gone to as children, if the job was offered her. Milly said she wanted to be free the coming year and that there would be plenty to do yet that fall on their ranch.

Fred began to feel ill-at-ease about that bump in his lap. It was really swelling up into something considerable. It began to hurt a little. At the same time an impulse to laugh began to work in Fred's belly. The way she was sitting on his lap their parts were only a couple of inches apart. If it weren't for their clothes, his underwear and trousers and her denim skirt and underpants, they could easy make connection in the dark of the car, possibly even all unbeknownst to duenna Cynthia, the old crab prune. Fred tried to withdraw his bump in between his thighs, but that had the effect of making his chest stick

246

out and pushing Milly forward on his lap.

The car kept dropping down into darkness and the long dark valley. Fred's ears cracked and slowly dulled over and cracked again. It was obvious they were descending rapidly. Staggered rock walls appeared on both sides of the road. The dark walls slowly closed in on them. Twice they crossed the river as it wound back and forth under the road. All four in the car fell silent. They watched the headlights spearing ahead through the bottom of the deep canyon.

They flashed under a log arch over the highway.

"What in the world was that?" Fred asked.

"Gallatin Gateway," Milly said.

"Then it shouldn't be too long before we hit Bozeman."

"That's right."

Fred was sure she felt him. And she didn't seem to mind. It was something she apparently expected from men and life. She sat quiet; no longer stirring on his lap. Fred asked, "Where do you folks live from Bozeman?"

"Northeast. We take the trail past Bridger Range."

Fred nodded. Too bad they weren't going west through Belgrade, only a dozen miles away. It looked like he'd have to call up his friend Don to come and get him from Bozeman.

The headlights of the coupe picked up standing water in the ditch on their right.

"Say, look at that," Fred said. He had to lean around Milly to see ahead.

"Irrigation ditch," Bud said. "Lots of irrigation through this part of the country."

Fred felt he should ask Milly to pardon him for that lump in his lap. It was the decent thing to do. There was no chance she hadn't noticed it. She couldn't possibly be so innocent as to think it was just some kind of bone

247

or odd knob on his thighbone. Around sheep she surely must have seen the ram in action. Farm kids, and certainly also ranch hands, had to know something about the mechanics of breeding. He had to figure out a way of saying he was sorry. In a dignified gentlemanly way. There had to be class in the way he remarked on it. That way she'd be sure to accept his apology, and forgive him.

"Milly?"

She turned her head, but kept her seat still. "Yes?"

"I . . . uhh . . ." Fred paused. Cynthia also turned her head a little to listen. Damn her. "Skip it."

Milly turned further. And stirred her seat on his bump. "Yes?"

"I'll tell you later. Though it's . . ." Fred stiffened upright. Ahead coming toward them was a pair of weaving carlights. "Say!"

"Yeh," Bud said, "I've had my eye on him. A darn drunk." Bud edged the coupe over on the shoulder of the road to give the oncoming car plenty of room to pass. The water in the irrigation ditch on the right glittered.

Fred slowly stiffened up under Milly, pressing his feet to the floorboards, thighs ridging up. The bump in his lap shriveled up. "If we can just pass them when they're on one of their zigs to our left."

"Yeh," Bud said. He too tightened up behind his wheel.

Cynthia shrank, lowering her head. Milly sat a little more upright than usual, with the air of a horsebacker about to leap her horse over a fence.

The paired headlights owled up bigger. They swung away and it looked for a moment the two Meade cars would get by.

But Bud had let the coupe slow down too much. The

248

oncoming car weaved back toward them. Everybody sucked a breath. The oncoming car just missed sideswiping the rear fender of the coupe. And then, like a great swallow, the coupe reared up, almost like a horse, there was a crash, the whut of a parting chain, and then the Chevy ran on, suddenly light and free. All four in the coupe made the motions of a rider on a jumping horse.

Both Milly and Fred whipped their heads around to look out through the back window. The oncoming car had caught the rear fender of the second Meade car. The headlights of the oncoming car whirled completely around one full turn and vanished; while the touring car jerked violently left and shot across the road into the dry ditch and hit the far embankment, radiator first, its rear wheels rising for a moment up in the air, pausing, and then dropping down. The impact had the effect of a catapult on the old couple. Ma Meade burst through the windshield; while Pa Meade, hanging onto the steering wheel, rose in the air to the full length of his arms, also whacked into the windshield, then dropped down in the seat again.

"My God!" Fred cried.

"Dad!" Milly cried.

Cynthia hunched herself up into a fetal position.

Bud jammed on the brakes and got the coupe stopped within a few rods. He grabbed up a flashlight and popped out of the car and darted back toward the stricken old couple. In the moment of trouble Bud was on the ball.

Milly, then Fred, popped out of the coupe too and were right on Bud's heels.

Bud's flashlight wiggled all over the touring car, found Pa Meade leaning over the steering wheel his face streaming blood, next picked out Ma Meade crumpled up on the embankment her left arm strangely angled up behind her head.

"Dad!" Milly cried again, and she went to him and put her arm around him.

Pa Meade slowly turned his bleeding face toward her. "Ma all right?"

"Ma!" Bud climbed up the embankment beside Ma Meade and gently rolled her over on her side.

Ma Meade smiled up at him. "Pa all right?"

Fred helped Milly help her father out of the car. All three stumbled over to where Bud held Ma Meade steady. Bud had trouble holding Ma Meade and the flashlight both. Fred took the flashlight and steadied its cone of light on Ma's strangely bent arm.

Pa Meade wiped blood out of his eyes. "You all right, Ma?"

Ma Meade's little smile crinkled up and became a look of pain. "I can't seem to manage my arm."

Bud quick held the arm. "Don't move it. It could be broke."

Ma Meade said then, quietly, "It is broke." She looked up at Pa Meade. "Anything broke on you, Pa?"

"No. Just got all this glass in my face."

"In your eyes?"

"No, just over my face."

Gradually all six became aware that behind them, in the opposite ditch where the irrigation water ran, there was a lot of wild cursing and splashing of water and even occasional hoarse laughter.

Fred shot the flashlight over at the other ditch. The oncoming car had landed in the water up to its windows. What looked like four soused frogs were floundering half in and half out of the car windows.

"Keep that light shining here," Milly commanded.

"Okay," Fred said. "I just wanted to make sure there

250

weren't any drowned rats over there."

"Rats is right," Milly said. "The drunks."

Bud was about pick up Ma Meade.

"Don't do that!" Fred said. "You might hurt her worse. Especially when something's broken. You shouldn't move such a person until you've at least made a splint. And checked her over for other broken bones."

"He's right," Milly said. "Just lay calm there, Ma, until we can flag down a car and ask them to get help."

Miraculously the paired lights of a car appeared from the west. Fred waved the flashlight up and down and sideways to wave down the car. The headlights enlarged; slowed; pulled over.

"My God," Bud said. "It's the sheriff. Now how could he have smelled out this accident so fast."

The sheriff got out of his car with a flashlight and came on the run. He was a very muscular fellow, with the full graceful movements of a wrestler. His badge flashed in the light. He sized things up in a whip, then called back to his car. "Jerry, get high behind and call out the ambulance."

Jerry inside the car slid over under the wheel and with a roar was off.

The sheriff flashed his light over both Pa and Ma Meade again. "Don't move her. But the old man here . . . have you got some bandages? Any kind of cloth?"

Milly said, "Well, not in . . . no." And then with quiet dignity reached under her denim skirt and slipped down her underpants, stepped out of it, and handed it to the sheriff. The sheriff blinked a second; handed Fred his flashlight; then began clearing off Pa Meade's face. He was careful not to get any blood on his tan uniform. Pa Meade suffered the sheriff's ministration with closed eyes.

Presently the sheriff said, "I don't think he's hurt all that bad. Surface cuts, mostly." He dabbed some more. He said down to Pa Meade, "You've got good blood, sir. It's already stopped bleeding." He said to Fred, "A little more light under his ear here."

As Fred held both lights on Pa Meade the thought shot through his head that it was too bad Milly couldn't be sitting on his lap now.

"Good," the sheriff said. "Now let's go over and look at the other car and its occupants." The sheriff took back his flashlight.

The four soused gentlemen in the other car turned out to be unhurt. They'd just had a good bump and then an inadvertent bath. Three of them were cussing the fourth member for being a lousy driver. It developed after some talk that the four men were members of a dance band and they were on their way to a dance hall at the Gallatin Gateway. And yes they had been drinking a little, though the driver the least.

"Bull," the sheriff said. "I'm booking you guys. What's the name of your band?"

"The Bozeman Boys."

It made Fred smile. In the Dutch language the word "boze" meant "bad, evil."

It didn't take Jerry, the deputy sheriff, long to get help. An ambulance came roaring out and two white-clad medics picked up Pa and Ma Meade and hustled them off to the hospital. Shortly after a farmer came puttputting up with a Fordson tractor and fished the dance band car out of the irrigation ditch. The farmer also pulled the Meade touring car out of the dry ditch.

On the way into town, Milly turned on Fred's lap. "That reminds me. There's a law in this state against picking up vagrants."

"That's right," Bud said. "And the sheriff is bound to

252

ask who Fred is. Because Fred is a witness."

A chill settled in Fred. His delight in having Milly sit on his lap without her pants was backfiring on him.

Milly smiled down at Fred. "Well, as for me, I'm saying Fred is a friend."

Cynthia was curiously silent, withdrawn. During all the commotion she had not got out of the coupe.

Bud glanced at Milly a moment; then went back to steering the car. "Okay by me. Because if we don't agree on that, the sheriff might also pinch us for picking Fred up."

"That's what we'll do then," Milly said.

Later, in the sheriff's office, after they had all given their version of what happened, Milly drew Fred to one side, "I suppose you'll be going on to Belgrade."

"Yes. I'm going to call my friend Don in a minute."

She smiled up at him. "Well, if you ever get out this way again, be sure to look us up."

"I will."

"Good-bye. And good luck."

"Bye, Milly."

It came to him while he was phoning Don that she hadn't given him her address. He'd also failed to pay close attention when Milly and Bud gave their home address to the sheriff.

Too bad.

Several days later, on the way back to Iowa, Don stopped in Sundance to get some gas. While Don had his old Ford serviced, Fred went over and sat on a big stone alongside the road and added some more lines to his poem about Yellowstone National Park:

> "Weary one day
> Of haying in the slough
> And slopping dumb hogs,

253

I got out my thumb
And became a vagabond.
I hitched, I walked,
I slept on open prairies,
I begged, I took,
I drove for an old maid,
I hitched a ride with a mad man,
I held a girl on my lap —
Oh, I traveled far and wide."

Otherwise, nothing much happened on the way home. A few smiles with Don, some jokes, a few laughs. And one prayer after an evening meal — in a restaurant yet.

Back on Pa's yard, after friend Don had driven on to Calvin College Seminary, Pa had a question for Fred. "Well, did you get to see your Shining Mountains?"

"Sure did."

"What was they like?"

"Like as if you was to tip up this land on a slant from here to Canton, until Canton would be two miles high."

"Gotske!"

"It's always cold that high up so there's snow all year round. That's what makes 'em shine."

"Thanks. We got enough snow here winters on the prairies."

"It's a great sight though, Pa."

"Huh. This rolling country is plenty good enough for me."

"In some places the earth rises straight up."

"Naw."

"Yep. When you stand at the foot of one of those cliffs and look up you almost fall over on your back."

Pa had one more question. "Are you sure you wasn't fooled into seeing what you saw because you was standing on your head and had a rush of blood to your brains? You always was peculiar in wanting to see things in a different way from the rest of us."

Fred laughed. "Well, maybe I was. I guess it does depend on where you stand and how you look at it."